FAWCETT ON ROCK

FAWCETT ON ROCK

Ron Fawcett and John Beatty
with Mike Harrison

UNWIN HYMAN
London   Sydney

First published in Great Britain by
Unwin Hyman, an imprint of Unwin Hyman Limited 1987

UNWIN HYMAN
Denmark House, 37–39 Queen Elizabeth Street, London SE1 2QB
and
40 Museum Street, London WC1A 1LU

Allen & Unwin (Australia) Ltd, 8 Napier Street, North Sydney,
NSW 2060, Australia

Allen & Unwin with the Port Nicholson Press, 60 Cambridge Terrace,
Wellington, New Zealand

ISBN 0 04 440076 4

British Library Cataloguing in Publication Data

Fawcett, Ron
    Fawcett on rock
    1. Rock climbing
    I. Title   II. Harrison, Mike
    796.5′223   GV200.2

Designed by Julian Holland
Typeset by Cambridge Photosetting Services
Printed and bound in Great Britain by Scotprint Ltd, Musselburgh

Mike Harrison has spent a lot of time talking to Ron about
his climbing, and accompanying him to Derbyshire crags.
This book is the synthesis of their conversations: all the ideas
and techniques are Ron's own, though the words and
expressions are Mike's.

Fawcett on Rock is *not* a beginners' guide to the sport. The
techniques described should only be practised by
intermediate and advanced climbers.

CONTENTS

Introduction:
No Pain. No Gain

Stoney Middleton Dale: a thicket of straggly elder, ugliest of winter trees, screens the rock buttress from the road. Thirty yards away lorries clank past, laden with aggregate, bottoming on their springs. Vegetation encroaches on to the limestone walls from either side – ash, hawthorn and ivy. A cold fret of mist, characteristic of March days in the Derbyshire Dales, hangs in the breeze and a scurf of dust from the quarreys opposite settles on dark leaves. The rock face is an open angle fifty feet high. The left wall overhangs, the right is slabby and smooth. Its colour varies from a chalky grey through beiges to patches of bright ochre. Dark stains weep from discontinuous cracks. The tide-marked hole of a cave entrance punctuates the base. A semi-circle of ground under the cliff is glutinous with mud, islanded with fertilizer bags, squares of carpet, filthy towels. It is the most unprepossessing of gymnasiums.

But that is exactly what it is, and on this cold grey morning there are eight gymnasts working out here at a changed sport. Two of them are wearing shorts, the others candy-striped or floral Lycra tights, or more sober tracksuit bottoms. A ghetto-blaster is thumping and tinning away, propped against a tree stump out of the mire: 'Relax, don't do it . . .'. Three of the climbers are in various states of dependence on ropes hanging down the cliff. Two more stand at the bottom belaying, one watches, a couple more boulder across the foot of the less steep wall. Of the eight, five are tall and slim, long-limbed and lightly-muscled; the other three are muscular and compact. Concentration is so intense that a general silence prevails, broken by sporadic supportive comment: 'It's just a bit of oomph – once you know it's really good, you just spring up.' Or again: 'Just push right up on that hand and slap for the jug. Go on . . !'

The climber who voices the latter encouragement, oldest of the group, is himself thirty feet up and midway through a sequence of 6b moves. Even at ground level an untrained body would barely be able to hang on holds of this smallness on rock at this angle – let alone reach them, rest there, then move on through. This gymnast, this athlete, however, completes the climb, abseils down, replaces a sliding self-protection device on the rope, and then repeats the whole process before taking a brief rest. After five such sets – five hundred feet of climbing up a severely overhanging wall on the smallest of finger pockets and edges – he will allow himself a break.

He squats by a tree, rolls a cigarette, watches the other climbers at work on the wall. After five minutes he sets to again, traversing this time across the base of the steeper wall – across, back, across again, his breathing exaggerated now, sharp exhalations. Eventually he drops off, ruefully rubbing his finger ends, and turns to speak: 'It feels as though my biceps are going to explode when I pull on that', he explains, pointing to the hold at which he jumped off. The move to which it is crucial is across a scooped hollow in the rock. There are no real footholds, just the friction of rubber pressed on dimpled patches in the slick surface. The hold in question is a shallow pocket, three-quarters-of-an-inch deep and an inch-and-a-half across, sloping, damp, and rimed with a chalky paste. He demonstrates its use. Two fingers, with the thumb curled behind them, clip into it at the precisest of angles.

'Like this!'

He grimaces, blows air out of his lungs, feeds in the power, and completes the move. 'No pain, no gain,' he gasps, before stepping lazily off on to a boulder and suggesting a cup of tea in the cafe down the dale.

The commanding figure in this performance is Ron Fawcett, the outstanding figure in the revolution which has taken place in the sport of rock climbing in Britain over the last fifteen years. He was born in the West Riding of Yorkshire, at the little village of Embsay, three miles out of Skipton, in 1955 – the year in which Joe Brown reached the summit of Kanchenjunga and Don Whillans made the first ascent of *Woubits* on Clogwyn Du'r Arddu.

He was the second of five children in a family of Yorkshire Dales farming stock, and has the 'mould of man, big-boned and hardy-handsome' of those people. His hands in particular are huge and powerful – almost to the point of being a standing joke in the climbing world, with tales abounding of visiting Japanese enthusiasts as eager and clamorous to see the outsize Fawcett fingers as earlier pilgrims must have been over saints' relics. Other tales tell of his being reduced to desperate straits by thin finger cracks or small limestone pockets, accessible to ordinary-sized fingers. That's one side of the benefit/detriment equation. Massively outweighing it on the other is the obvious strength and durability of his physique. Almost alone amongst his own and later generations of rock-gymnasts and athletes (in no sense is the term of mere rock-climber adequate to the activity in which he's engaged), he is untroubled by the crippling finger-tendon and shoulder injuries which others have suffered.

He first intruded himself on the attention of the climbing public through an article published in *Mountain* magazine at New Year, 1972. Dave Cook, writing on 'The Sombre Face of Yorkshire Climbing', introduced him as follows:

'My mind, remembering the days when a long Ogwen apprenticeship preceded VS climbing, also boggles at the speed at which young climbers race up the grades. Ron Fawcett from Skipton was fifteen when I met him in Ilkley Quarry soloing HVS routes. He was already doing first ascents of this standard on limestone. His walk home from school led him beneath a limestone quarry on which he constructed an alternative path of VS standard in order to vary his homeward route.'

Down in the cafe in Stoney Middleton Dale during the break from his training, Ron himself talked about his beginnings:

'As a kid I used to play in Rock Wood, across the road from our house. My mate Martin Brewster (he's dead big now – like his pop! It's frightening to see the lads I was at school with) and I used to get up to all the usual things – climbing trees, making swings, lighting fires,

Crimping on Millstone Edge.

making bombs out of weed-killer and sugar. There were some big limestone slabs in the wood which used to be popular – it's called Haw Bank Quarry. We used to see fellows with ropes and bright clothes there at weekends. We were too stroppy to ask them if we could join in, so we used to roll rocks down on them or solo the things they were doing – I was a right little tearaway. One day Brewster decided he was going to run down one of these slabs. It was about 100 ft. He set off but he'd forgotten about the barbed wire fence at the bottom. He made a right mess of himself and got a real bollocking off his mum.

There was a climbing club at our school, but they wouldn't let me go at all, because the Games Master ran it and I never liked team games. I like to do it myself rather than depend on other people. I did go to the Lake District with the school, walking, though. We walked up Coniston Old Man and saw climbers on Dow Crag. That really impressed me – to a youth Dow Crag looks absolutely enormous. I fancied having a go, and in November or December, 1970, I got to know about a group of Venture Scouts that met in a cottage in Skipton Bus Station. The first time I ever went out was with a lad called Arthur Champion. He was about five years older than me and a really good caver. He said he'd take me out one Saturday, told me to turn up and bring a pair of pumps. We went up to Rylestone and did a few Severes, than I led a VS. It had a hard start but was easier above. That was my first proper day's climbing, and the next day we went to Malham, which seemed more of an adventure.'

The enterprise, determination and distance from convention displayed here are characteristic of the entry into the sport of most of the really great climbers. That the young Fawcett had the commitment and drive which are perhaps the most important factors in achieving that status was soon readily apparent. Here is Dennis Gray with an early reminiscence:

'I held a housewarming party in Guiseley at which there were people like Nat Allen and Speedy Smith. Bev Barratt, a local youth club leader and Yorkshire climber, brought Ron along because he wanted him to meet these famous climbers. The next day a group of us old men and some younger climbers, including Ron, went bouldering at Caley – it was a terrible day, wintertime and wet and cold. I remember Ron climbing on a boulder called the Sugar Loaf. At that time he was not by any means the best of the young climbers in the group – there were others with more natural ability than him – but I can remember his great determination. There was one particular problem which Speedy Smith had done in these streaming conditions – we were all climbing in big boots in the pouring rain. Ron, in something like a pair of Tuf Boots, just made it. He

forced himself up this thing and all the other young climbers backed right off.'

Within six months of starting to climb, Ron was starting to seek out the new routes, or the free ascents of the old aid climbs:

'Being a young whippersnapper and wanting to get in on the action, I attempted to free climb *Mulatto Wall* at Malham. On the first pitch I attempted to clip the bolt with an overlarge krab. It would not go in and I could not go up so down I flew, ripping out all my gear, making a hole in a tree and knocking out my second as we collided. I had my helmet on at the time. A week later I returned with a stitched hand . . .'

This time he succeeded on the route. Another incident from the same period reveals the same combination of fortitude, application and luck. It took place on Kilnsey, the great overhaning buttress of limestone in Wharfedale. One of the practices of the group of climbers Ron had joined was to spend much of the winter on the big aid routes with which the major Yorkshire crags abound. The efficient rope handling these demanded, along with the breathtaking situations into which they lead, were both important elements in a young climber's apprenticeship.

On this occasion he was alone, playing truant from school (having thrown his climbing gear from his bedroom window in the morning and picked it up on the way out so that his mother wouldn't know):

'I went to solo the *Superdirect*, which is the hard one across the roof at Kilnsey. I had two short ropes, probably 100 ft or so. I got round the roof, abseiled down and pulled myself into the stance, then seconded the pitch on prusik loops. There was a free-climbing pitch to finish, it was pissing with rain, and I didn't want to miss the school bus back down to Skipton. So I abseiled off but the ropes ended forty feet short of the ground. I tied a knot in one of the ropes and abseiled on to it, letting the other go. It took about five feet to burn through the bit of bootlace I'd used as a belay sling on the pegs above, so I fell over thirty feet and hit the grass bank below – I used to be able to land well. Anyway, I then set off rolling down the bank and ended up cocooned in the rope in the beck below the crag. I nearly drowned.'

It needs to be understood that the regionalism of British climbing (thanks to the magazines and greater mobility of climbers the situation obtains to nothing like the same extent today) in earlier decades had led to some remarkable aberrations in local gradings of climbs. Yorkshire limestones, on which Ron's early attentions were mainly focused, was more competitively graded perhaps than any other rock-type in the country. There were VS's on Malham which were technically 6a, and which would have been given

Extremely Severe in any other region. If a climber was going to survive in this hard school, he was going to improve very rapidly indeed. Just how rapidly is illustrated by an account given by Al Evans of his first meeting, in the Lake District, with Ron. Again, weather is an important factor – before climbing walls and training in gyms had their present currency it was fairly commonplace for climbers to moderate their ambitions and ascend a token route in the rain:

'It was a miserably wet Sunday and we decided to splash up one of the easy route on Castle Rock of Triermain before going home. When we got there Ron was on *The Ghost*, which was probably the hardest routes on the crag at the time. I felt quite worried for him, because although the traverse is safe enough, on the top arête there's no protection. Anyway, he did it straight off, no trouble.

Afterwards we got talking to him and asked him what he was doing on that sort of route in this weather. Apparently someone had told him that Lake District Extremes were easy, which some of them are, but instead of going on to one of the easy ones he'd gone straight on to *The Ghost*, which definitely isn't. We could see he was young, but just how young we didn't realize – he'd be about fifteen at the time.'

It is natural in the sport for climbers to get to hear about, and team up with, their peers. The few who do not are invariably, and often with very good reason, treated with suspicion. Probably Ron's only peer in the country at the time was Peter Livesey, a fellow Yorkshireman and one of the most extraordinary characters ever to have graced and inspired the climbing world. Livesey, in his late twenties when he came to prominence in climbing, was the most rigorous of trainers – he virtually introduced the concept of training along athletic lines to the climbing world (though others, notably Colin Mortlock at the beginning of the sixties, had attempted to do the same before him and been laughed aside by the temper of the times). He was also the slyest of tacticians – question marks crowded in his wake like hens cackling over spilt grain. An enigmatic smile and a Gallic shrug were his usual response. His legacy was a stunning roll-call of the great routes which stimulated climbing's mid-seventies revolution: *Face Route, Footless Crow, Claws, Right Wall, Cream, Fingerlicker, Downhill Racer, Wellington Crack* – all of them still test-pieces for the aspiring extremist.

'I knew from when I first climbed with him that Ron was better than me,' he jokes. 'The thing was, not to let Ron know that.'

It was not a fact which could long be kept hidden. Ethical pressures intruded as well – an argument, for example, over whether or not a sling had been used on a particular first ascent. The partnership, without any

Soloing *Left Ski Track*, 5.11, Joshua Tree, California.

great degree of acrimony on either side, fell apart. But not before it had given Ron the confidence to know that he was up there with the best, and that any existing route in the country was now within his powers. If Livesey had been the father-figure, the Old Testament God full of flaws, character, humour and magnificence, Ron was the young prophet of the New Testament, and his creed was purism.

It *was* a creed as well in the mid-seventies, and forcefully expressed. There were the old Yorkshire aid routes to be free-climbed. There were the impure routes of others to be cleaned up and commented upon in the magazines. In article after article his now-proven ability gave him the confidence to castigate the less praiseworthy activities of his predecessors and contemporaries:

'Undoubtedly there are some brilliant routes in Wales, but a lot of them fall short of the ethical purity line. Really fine routes like *Resurrection* and *Grasper* were sadly over-aided by their first ascentionists and considered free routes, only to be cleaned in later ascents.'

Judgements on individual routes took the same severe line:

Medi: 'Climbed originally with a tension move and peg.'
Resurrection: 'Rather overaided on its first ascent.'
Wellington Crack: 'regrettably used a sling for aid near the top.'
Great Arête: 'An overpowering line that was pegged into submission by Drummond, later free-climbed by Livesey and Foster.'
The Moon: 'another Drummond attempt, was another to succumb to a later pure ascent.'

His assessments of the quality of routes were no less terse:

Positron: 'rather overrated.'
Creeping Lemma: 'vastly overrated.'
Ordinary Route: 'hardly a brilliant line.'

Obviously, statements as rigorous as these demanded individual achievement to back them up. The lines were still there to be climbed, albeit at a higher standard than had yet been fully achieved. One of them was at the Cow and Calf Rocks, just outside Ilkley, where in 1978 the 23-year-old Fawcett was taking a teacher-training course. A 60 ft long overhanging crack, starting in insignificance and widening beyond a half-height four-foot roof to unuseability, it had been pronounced by Livesey to be 'too hard for now.' Fawcett's willingness to suffer for his art comes out strongly in his description of its first ascent:

'. . . on a rather damp Saturday morning a tense leader launched out. It just had to go. My meaty, overlarge fingers are stuffed into tiny cracks, skin tearing, until they find a slot that accepts them up to the first joint. The crack then kinks slightly and narrows nastily; the line of holds leading to the roof is out of reach . . . a move in desperation, cramming poor digits in to the end of the nail, sees me panting under the roof. My forearms ache as I hang sloth-like from the lip, a runner sinking like a dream but my jams not.

I try to get my foot round the lip, but no go. My arms don't obey and they let me fall – only a short drop but pride is hurt and I storm back up in rage. I can feel every heartbeat as my jaded muscles try hard to do their stuff. I sweat and curse, and just as I'm all-in the jams sink. Well done, arms, you deserve a medal!'

Throughout the late seventies and early eighties Fawcett was the ubiquitous, unrivalled Master of British rock. There were other notable figures around – Pat Littlejohn continued to produce major classic lines throughout the country, Pete Whillance specialized in cool, remote leads, and John Redhead was spectacularly audacious on the thin wall-climbs of Wales. But it was Fawcett who dominated, and who opened up the blank walls of difficulty's new order: the Vector Buttress headwall taken by *Strawberries* (1980); the series of routes in the remaining bare spaces on the walls of Cenotaph Corner, particularly that to the left of Livesey's *Right Wall* which gave *Lord of the Flies* (1979); the bleak stretch of white rock beneath Anglesey's North Stack lighthouse, up the centre of which went *The Cad* (1978), where two controversial bolts were placed for protection; the smooth verticality between *Gargoyle* and *Octo* above Clogwyn Du'r Arddu's East Gully where *Psychokiller* (1980) found a way; the technically desperate and ferociously overhanging twin starts to Gordale's *Cave Route* (1982). And perhaps above all, the soaring lean of Derbyshire's Raven Tor – in the words of one magazine writer of the mid-seventies 'the ultimate outcrop [which] defies all attempts at free-climbing it'. Fawcett climbed seven routes here between 1976 and 1982, culminating in *The Prow*, still regarded as one of the desperates, 'the ultimate body-pump'.

Chris Gore, who was a front-runner in the pack which began to catch up with Ron in 1982, makes the following assessment of his contribution to climbing up to that time:

'The thing was that after Livesey faded out it was always Ron who was pushing his own standard, and that's the hardest thing in the world to do. In running you have pacemakers, but he had no-one but himself. What he did, despite that handicap, was absolutely brilliant and will be looked on as one of the watersheds in years to come.'

The year 1982 is significant in that a rival for the crown emerged. The following year this young pretender, Jerry Moffat, firmly seized the initiative with his ascents of *Revelations*, a technical masterpiece which created a direct start to *The Prow* on Raven Tor, and *Master's Wall* on Clogwyn Du'r Arddu, a long and serious lead which had been bravely contested by John Redhead prior to Moffat's ascent. Not only had Moffat taken the initiative, but in 1983 Fawcett was put abruptly and seriously out of the action. He had been working on a television broadcast from Dinas Cromlech on a wet day, and in the evening, restless as ever when under-exercised, he went up to Clogwyn y Grochan alone for a work-out:

'It was a dismal evening, the crag deserted, routes with crucial holds coated in slime, jams sliding down wet cracks. Darkness. I was woken by the dog licking my face. All around were jagged boulders spattered with blood; my left hand had no support; it hung limp and hurt like hell. I wrenched it into some sort of shape,

First ascent of *Desperate Dan* E7 6c, Ilkley, Yorkshire.

which nearly made me pass out, stuffed it into my pocket, and walked to Llanberis.

A broken radius and ulna put me out of business for quite a while . . .'

This was by no means the only broken limb in Ron's career – the number of those runs into double figures. But it was one of the worst, and psychologically it came at a crucial time. What follows gives the measure of the man – his ability to rise to the challenge when it presents itself. Ron was seriously injured. Moffat was acclaimed as, and revelling in the position of, the New Star, and was casting his eye around for suitable new conquests. One of the most obvious lines in the country was the arête to the right of *Green Death* on Derbyshire's Millstone Edge. It was virtually holdless, protectionless apart from the possibility of placing a camming device in one of two old quarryman's shot-holes too low down to give much security on the crux moves. Extensive practice on a rope enabled Moffat to climb it without top-rope tension and pronounce it possible. He then declared his intention of returning to make the first ascent when the good weather came, and proclaimed that whoever led it on sight would have to be The Master. When he climbed it, therefore, he would name it *The Master's Edge*.

Fawcett meanwhile, the break healed, was training obsessively to regain his fitness. In December 1983, he climbed a series of extremely difficult new problems on gritstone, his account of one of which conveys the intensity he was bringing to the task:

'I could always come back tomorrow. In ten minutes I could be by the fire with a brew. One last try. I committed myself. One move from the break and an impasse; no way could I climb down and by now I was too far up to jump. Go for it, but with which hand? My fingers burnt with the pain of that edge but I kept on cranking way past the level of acceptable pain . . .'

On December 29th, he drove up to Millstone and inspected Moffat's unled line. He set off up the bottom section, arranged some protection in the shot-hole, and moved on past it:

'Smearing with my feet I snatched the arête and put my right toe in the top hole. My left toe went on to the arête and I pressed hard. It had picked up some lichen and it shot off. I followed it. The runners held and I was lowered to the ground. I chalked up and got straight back on it. Up to the holes it was much less gripping but harder because I had blocked the bottom one up with a runner. Once established at my high point the motor drives started firing. I laybacked the arête in classic style. Somehow I got my foot on a very sloping edge on the arête ten feet above the holes. I started gibbering. Only two moves to a jug. Could I step up and reach it or was it too far? Failure would be painful to say the least.

The hell with it. I stepped up and grabbed.

It was all over, bar the shouting . . .'

At the time of writing, more than three years on, *The Master's Edge* has been repeated only once, in the course of which ascent the leader, Mark Leach, took a long fall from high up on the route. The steely impetus and total commitment of Fawcett's ascent underline the fact that, although he may now have a peer group around him, he is still unquestionably one of the great climbers of this (or any) era of climbing history. There is a sense in which, with *The Master's Edge*, Ron finally arrived at a true public estimate of his vast talent and enthusiasm for, as well as dedication and contribution to, his chosen sport.

Let's pick him up again where we left him a few thousand words ago, in Stoney Middleton Cafe. He's finished a meagre lunch of tea and a sticky bun, smoked a few roll-ups, and the sun's filtering through, promising warm rock on the gritstone edges. So it's up to the west-facing slabs of Froggatt for the afternoon session. Once there, the sun breaks through and he takes off his shirt to bask in it, lean-bodied, with great ropes of muscle at the rear of the rib-cage on either side. They stand out in perfect definition as he soloes, relaxedly, contemplatively, up Livesey's route *Downhill Racer* (E4, 6a), feet angling on to the quarter-inch sloping holds with careful precision, then down *Long John's Slab* (E3, 5c), up *Hairless Heart* (E5, 5c) and down *Synopsis* (E2, 5c). Bouldering, he strolls, hands off the rock, across the old 6a moves of *Joe's Problem*. His body instinctively places itself in the correct positions. He comments, on the grades of the Extremely Severe routes around which he's wandering at will, that 'I can't make a proper judgement and I don't think the people who write the guidebooks can either,' and further berates the guide writers in saying that 'when I was doing my 100 Extremes in a day on grit, the main difficulty was finding the routes from the guide.' Bare-chested, despite snow still lying in patches on the ground, he smiles at the thought that 'they'll all be back in Sheffield whingeing about how cold it is today.' You watch him with an underlying awareness that his eleven-and-a-half stone of lightness, elegance and microdot foot-precision could so easily – has too often – become so much dead weight hurtling into the boulders. Yet the compulsion lives on. On *Artless* (E4, 6b) he looks down after completing the crux, and musingly tells that 'I hate that – it's one of my little purges that I make myself do it. I always feel so gangly on it. If I find it hard to reach the holds, and I'm six-foot-three, how the fuck did Whillans do it?'

The respect for the great pioneers, and his own innate

Soloing *Edge Lane* E5 5c, Millstone Edge.

modesty continually shine through. As does his pleasure and enthusiasm: 'All these numbers, all this talk about what grade they are, as if it matters. Why does nobody talk about quality any more. Why don't they realize just how good it is just to be out here. . . ?'

On the technical side of rock climbing, what follows is probably the best treatise ever written. Yet the single last comment above is the most important that its author makes. It amplifies, underscores, and to a large extent explains Ron Fawcett's continuing greatness as a climber. Learn what you can from his enormous technical expertise, but bear that simple philosophy with you as you do so. It's the key to the real enjoyment of the sport. And enjoy it I hope you do.

Jim Perrin
Criccieth 1987

Pichenibule, Verdon Gorge.

Ron Fawcett: Rock Climber
Acknowledgement . . . by John Beatty

The winch weighed a hundredweight and was bolted to the bedrock. Chris flicked the ratchet lock, Sid began his descent of the gorge wall. The telephone safety rope gave him access to the cable party above for the required speed and eventual position on the enormous impending walls that flanked the crack. Below him swept the 1,300 foot *Voie de la Demande,* a classic free-climb in the Gorge du Verdon. Hanging comfortably in his belay seat entwined in safety ropes and wires and swinging gently in the warm morning updraft, a full 300 feet from the gorge summit he could now fully concentrate on his subject.

Ron had climbed the lower section alone in the cool dawn air, and now, patiently bridged across the upper chimney cracks shaded from the sun, awaited Sid's call for action. In a sun-baked arena, the only sounds were the quiet whirring of a camera and wall creepers fluttering in shafts of hot light. Ron breathed evenly, stretching and reaching with little effort across the notorious smooth and overhanging cleft, completely alone, completely in control. Star bridged above the gaping air, his powerful movements deceptive in their apparent ease, he held still for a moment, motionless high above the silver stream way below in the gorge. He climbs on. A twig snaps and I shudder as my rope

springs tight. Ron with no rope is utterly committed, climbing fluently and free. We are not there, only the rock is there, and the morning sunshine and the unfettered joy of it.

Rock climbing is many things to many people, a game, a trick, a dangerous courtship a sense of rightness and fun. For Ron it is all of these and more, it is his passion and his style.

I hope this book helps to show more clearly the extraordinary art of rock climbing today as personified by one of its greatest exponents. It has been my pleasure to illustrate in colour some of the atmosphere surrounding Ron's climbing. I would like to extend my thanks to Jim Perrin for his care in preparing the introduction, to Mike Harrison for his enthusiasm and control of the main text, to Canon Cameras for their confidence in my work, and principally to Ron and Gillian for their entire cooperation in this project, and for the sheer fun of it all.

At the top of the gorge that morning, Ron pulled strongly off the top move to perfectly flat rock. The scented air was heating up, the crickets were whizzing the day away. It was not to the assembled company he turned, but a few quiet steps away, to a spot on the edge, to sit down with legs dangling and to gaze out, and to feel the rock and the space again and again.

Soloing *La Demande*, Verdon Gorge, being filmed by
Sid Perou.

Above: *Pichenibule*, Verdon
Gorge, 7c (French grade).

Left: *Edge Lane*, Millstone Edge,
E5 6a.

Left: *Pichenibule*, Verdon Gorge.

Above: *Sardine*, E5 6b,
Raven Tor.

Above: *Master's Edge*, E7 6c,
Millstone Edge.

Left: *Bareback Rider*, 6a boulder
problem, the Roaches.

Below and Opposite:
Revelations, E7 6c, Raven Tor.

Above and Opposite: *Bastille*, E6 6b, High Tor.

Left: *Courage Fuyons*, Buoux (7a French).

Above: *T.C.F.*, Buoux (6c French).

Cave Route Righthand, Gordale Scar, E6 6b.

Top of *Pierrepoint*, Gordale Scar, E7 6c 6b.

Cave Route Righthand,
Gordale Scar, E6 6b.

Right: *King Swing*, Malham
Cove, E6 6b.

Above: *Pierrepoint*, Gordale
Scar, E7 6c.

Above: *Zoolook*, Malham Cove,
E7 6c.

Left: *So High*, Joshua Tree,
(solo) B1 – California

Left and Above: Bouldering at
Almscliffe.

Left: *Wall of Horrors*, Almscliffe,
E3, 5c.

Above: *Western Front*,
Almscliffe, E2 5b.

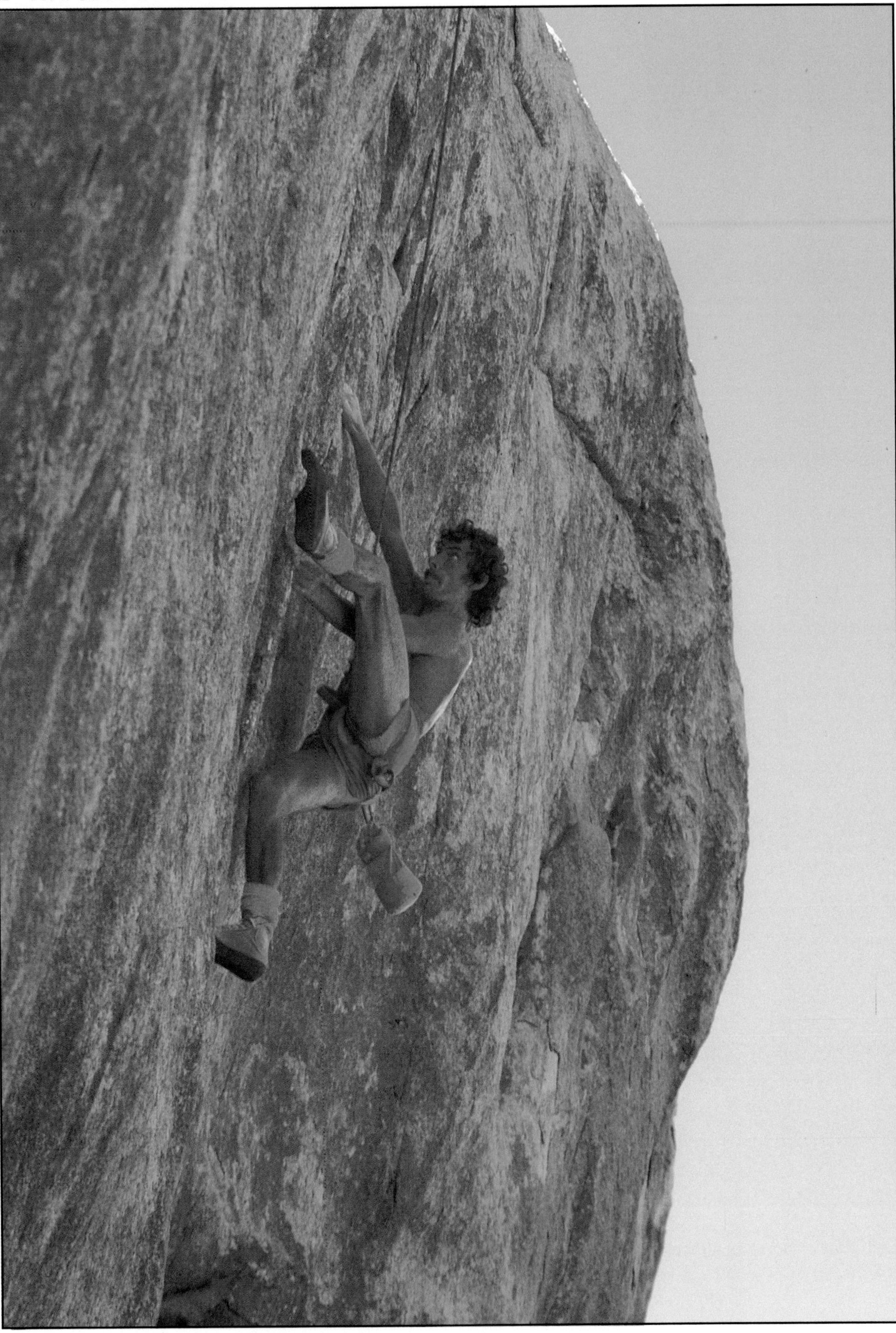

Left: *Baby Apes*, 5.12, Joshua
Tree, California

Above: *Camembert Fergusson*,
Buoux (French 7a)

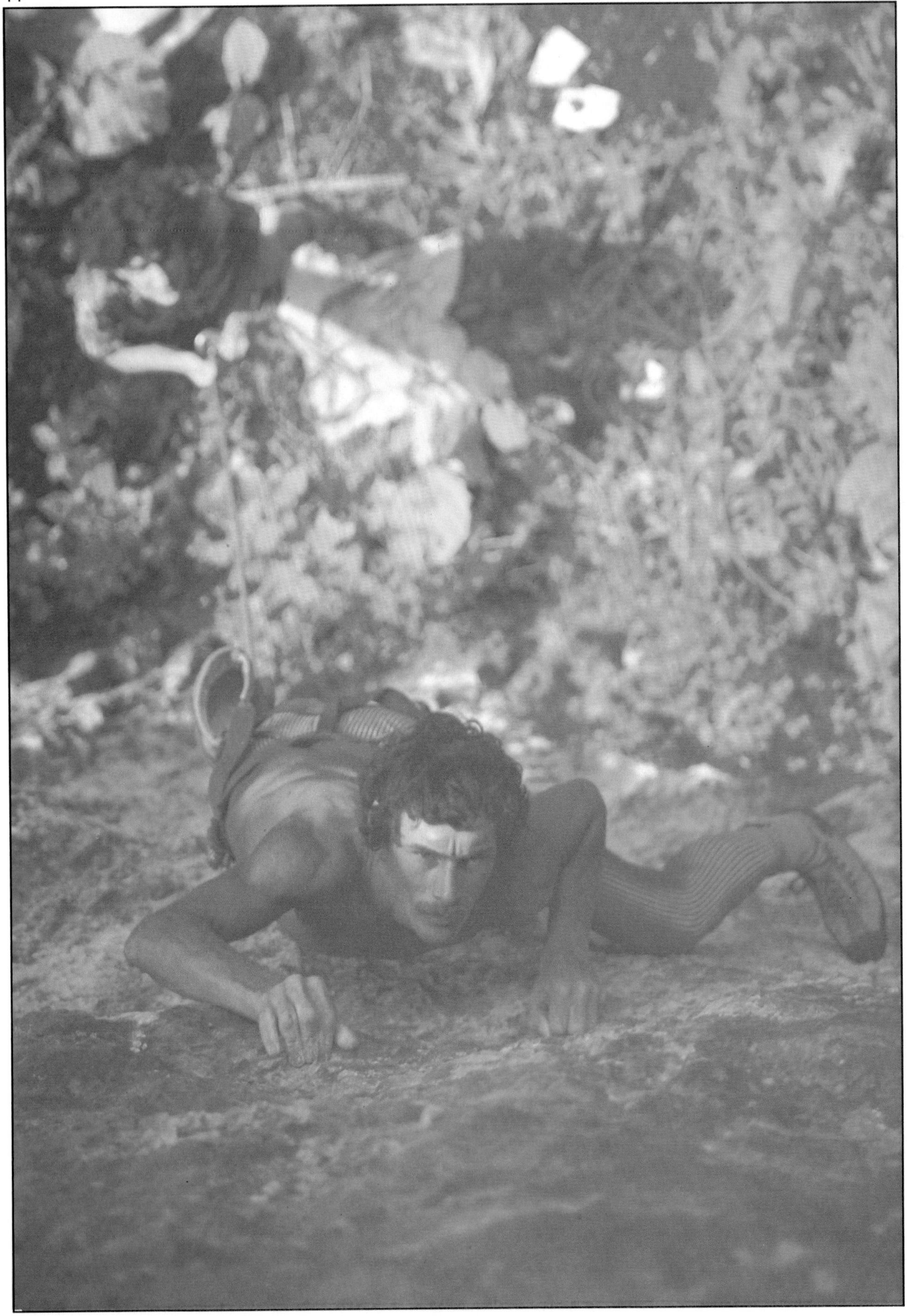

Opposite, Above and Top: *Ogre*,
Chee Tor, E7, 6c.

Above and Top: Trying to get the pictures for the technique section!

Right: Gill and Bill at Gordale Scar.

Froggatt pinnacle.

Introduction

THE CODE OF MISCONDUCT

I walked up to Froggatt through the beech trees on a warm September morning. Last year's leaves were scattered around in the shade of this year's. The woods had a cool smell. It was ideal weather for what I had in mind.

I train on them so often I sometimes see these gritstone edges when I close my eyes. Bored with wandering aimlessly along them from one route to another, I planned to solo a hundred extremes in the day. It was a loose plan. I would approach the edges in whatever order seemed attractive. On the map you can see them laid out along the contour from Curbar Gap to Moscar Fields, like curvature of the spine, cut at irregular intervals by the roads that lead to Sheffield. (Here in the northern section all roads lead to Sheffield: but not, you hope, to the Hallamshire Hospital.) A driver would have been useful, but I had decided to drive myself. There were two other clauses in my 'code of misconduct' for this episode: I could solo downward as well as up. And if doubt crept in on any move I could back off it without loss of face.

You begin as you mean to go on, I thought: so I got straight onto *Downhill Racer* from the eroded slot in the sand beneath, and came back down *Long John's Slab* next door. It was a way of announcing my intentions to myself. From there I worked leftwards, climbing from memory. The crag was deserted and nicely in the shade; the footage mounted up. *Tree Survivor, Oedipus, Cave Wall*: I was getting good friction, and I could feel my head settling in. Every so often I had a look down at the oaks and beeches, or across the valley to the limestone. After a bit I went back to my starting point and worked off in the opposite direction. The hard routes on *Great Slab* always seem a bit comfortless and bleak to a thug like me. They demand footwork: I prefer to get my fingers crimped round an edge or two. Nevertheless, I cleaned my boots and five routes later I had broken a psychological barrier without for once breaking a bone.

No bones broken, but I hadn't brought any dinner. By now the tourists would be wandering in a benign dream past the restaurant windows in Castleton; so instead of continuing south to Curbar I ran back down the hill and drove over to Hathersage; there, as well as something to eat, I could get a glimpse of the world of the sane, those marvellous creatures who don't feel it necessary to wreck themselves in search of a sensation or a crust or a tick in the guidebook. The streets were full of people. The waitresses were lovely. Where I

could have lingered, obsession pushed me out blinking into the sunshine and up the hill to Stanage Edge.

I know the Dangler area well. This enabled me to knock off half a dozen routes quite quickly, but after that I was concentrating hard. The thing is, I don't like Stanage all that much. All those classic severes like upright pianos in a twenties living room. All that lichen which makes you feel equally insecure whether it's wet and slimy or blowing about under your fingers like dust. Hence I didn't actually know a number of the routes – I would have to find and solo them on sight. The new guidebook, I discovered, runs from left to right; everybody else works the crag logically, from right to left . . . There was no time now to enjoy any of these climbs, to give them (and your own effort) a moment of contemplation when you reached the top. It was keep moving, keep concentrating, keep on the surface of the rock and leave its meaning until later. . . . By the time I reached *Archangel* I was pissed off. But then down among the boulders I spotted two familiar figures, Johnny Dawes and Martin Veale top-roping 'ultimate' arête problems, dabs of chalk on impossible holds. . .

I could have stayed all afternoon, safe on a top-rope or fielding the aerodynamic Dawes, but an obsession is an obsession. After *Wall End* I realized I was spending more time finding routes than climbing them, and by *Counts Buttress* I'd had enough. I ran back along the top of the edge with increasingly sore feet.

Adrenalin and chocolate

In fact, it was going well. Three o'clock and fifty-seven extremes under my belt. I cheered up, got Lou Reed's 'New Sensations' blasting out of the car stereo, gulped

Above and Beyond, Burbage South, E3 6a.

crag was infested with midges. My idea was to move so fast they wouldn't have the time to bite. It didn't work. As I moved leftwards along the edge they were giving me more trouble than the climbs. I met John Allen, taking a friend up *Kayak*; we had a chat but the light was going and things were getting tight; I still had twenty routes to go. By the time I reached *Apollo Buttress* the lights were on down in the dale so I ditched my shirt and ran down to the Deadbay area. After that it was one last sprint to mop up the remaining lines round *Apollo*, leaving my favourite little problems till last.

They floated by in a dream as the sun went below the horizon.

The temperament of opposites

At the beginning of the day I had put a cigar and a box of matches in my chalk bag. They were still there. Stretched out on the rough gritstone, watching the smoke go straight up into the air, I could let the day wash over me, think about a pint of Tetley's, and review what I'd done.

Most climbers would see the attraction of the challenge. A few might even envy me the time to do something like this – the same ones, paradoxically, who would think of it as just another stunt, publicity for the professional rock-jock out to earn his crust. But despite the fact that my final list contained three E5s and several E4s, no climber would ever use the word 'suicidal' or 'irresponsible' about the project.

Climbing, after all, is climbing. Whatever your personal standard, when you solo the risk is maintained. And I had set myself that code of misconduct when I set off: solo upwards or downwards but back off when things look doubtful.

Yet, under Froggatt at about eleven o'clock, just before I set out on *Hairless Heart*, I had passed the site of my last bad fall, trying not to remember myself as a crumpled mess on the floor, more bones broken than I wanted to count. On Stanage later in the day I had worn my oldest pair of Firés – so comfortable I needn't change in and out of training shoes to run between buttresses: but so battered I had to wrap carpet tape round them to keep them on my feet. Later still, driving to Burbage with the sunshine thudding on the roof of the car and Lou Reed thumping through my head, I had felt the adrenalin reaching levels to dazzle even the slyest of professionals. Finally at Curbar after eight hours with my brain clamped in a vice of concentration, I had watched the lights of my own village going on across the valley and wanted to go home. Instead, I half-climbed, half-fell down *Deadbay Crack* in the fading light, and, stumbling out of the dim earthy bowl at the bottom, carried on towards *Ulysses or Bust*. The code of misconduct had worn thin.

Sardine, E5 6b, Raven Tor, Derbyshire.

some orange juice and chocolate. The adrenalin was running and I was trying to think of Heinz jokes. I screeched into the car park at Burbage South, checked the guidebook out and dashed towards the dark slot of the quarries.

Burbage looks, they used to say, as if chickens had been over it. This says nothing about clean, demanding little routes which catch the light late in the day. I like that. The rock is cool, but you can soak up the evening sunshine. At Burbage the climbs have good names; they're varied and close together. *Above and Beyond, Pebble Mill*, a little easier now we have the sticky rubber, but both lovely, intricate sequences. I did sixteen more solos there, in an hour. It would be dark in two, and the final part of the programme was a bit vague. Millstone was closer: but I signed up for Curbar, and another hasty drive.

At Curbar the sun was hot, the air was still, and the

On the rock, climbers try to live intensely but not haphazardly. The two aims conflict, and reconciling them is the major reward of the sport. Pushing yourself to your mental and physical limits on a Saturday afternoon demands a temperament of opposites. The basis of this contract – between recklessness and care, innocence and experience, fear and pleasure – is confidence. Nothing gives you confidence like technique.

Superdirectissima, E4 6b, Kilnsey, Yorkshire.

100 – the list

FROGGATT EDGE

1.	Downhill Racer	17m	E4	6a
2.	Long Johns Slab	14m	E3	5c
3.	Tree Survivor	10m	E3	6a
4.	Oedipus	9m	E4	6b
5.	Cave Wall	11m	E3	5c
6.	Cave Crack	11m	E1	5c
7.	Heartless Hare	11m	E5	5c
8.	Great Slab	18m	E3	5b
9.	Artless	15m	E4	6b
10.	Hairless Heart	15m	E5	5c
11.	Synopsis	12m	E2	5c
12.	Nutty Land	15m	E1	5c
13.	Brown's Eliminate	14m	E1	5b
14.	Armageddon	14m	E2	5c
15.	Big Crack	15m	E1	5b
16.	Stiff Cheese	12m	E1	5c

STANAGE

17.	3D Wall	8m	E2	6a
18.	Tip Off	14m	E1	5b
19.	Dry Rot	13m	E1	5b
20.	Tippler	20m	E1	5b
21.	Tippler Direct	16m	E2	6a
22.	Dangler	16m	E2	5c
23.	Censor	15m	E3	5c
24.	Yosemite Wall	16m	E1	5b
25.	Topaz	10m	E4	6a
26.	Easter Rib	15m	E1	5b
27.	Ice Boat	20m	E1	5c
28.	Coconut Ice	18m	E2	5c
29.	The Actress	9m	E1	5b
30.	Desperation	12m	E1	5c
31.	Constipation	12m	E3	6a
32.	Wuthering	18m	E1	5b

33.	Asp	17m	E3	6a
34.	Dont Bark, Bite	18m	E1	5c
35.	Dark Continent	18m	E1	5c
36.	Acheron	17m	E1	5b
37.	Blood Shot	15m	E2	5b
38.	Old Dragon	12m	E1	5b
39.	Plastic Cream	10m	E1	5c
40.	Curving Buttress	16m	E2	5b
41.	Monday Blue	17m	E2	5b
42.	Left Unconquerable	17m	E1	5b
43.	Millsom's Minion	22m	E1	5b
44.	Crossover	12m	E3	5c
45.	Nuke the Midges	9m	E1	5c
46.	Esso Extra	17m	E1	5b
47.	Cinturato	14m	E1	5c
48.	Centaur	8m	E1	5c
49.	Living at Speed	8m	E1	5b
50.	Archangel	21m	E3	5b
51.	Giro	9m	E1	5c
52.	Argus	9m	E2	5b
53.	Shock Horror Slab	9m	E1	6b
54.	Counts Buttress	15m	E1	5b
55.	Daydreamer	9m	E2	6b
56.	Nightmare Slab	9m	E1	5c

BURBAGE SOUTH

57.	Millwheel Wall	9m	E1	5b
58.	Pretzel Logic	9m	E3	6a
59.	Zeus	11m	E2	5b
60.	Above and Beyond	6m	E3	6b
61.	Dork Child	8m	E1	5c
62.	Pebble Mill	11m	E4	6b
63.	Nick Knack	8m	E1	6a
64.	Old MacDonald	8m	E1	6a
65.	Sorb	9m	E2	5c
66.	Fade Away	8m	E1	6a

67.	Recurring Nightmare	8m	E4	6b
68.	The Knock	9m	E4	5c
69.	Yoghurt	14m	E3	6b
70.	The Boggart	12m	E2	6a
71.	Boggart Left Hand	12m	E2	5c

CURBAR EDGE

72.	Scroach	21m	E2	5c
73.	Left Eliminate	12m	E1	5c
74.	Right Eliminate	18m	E3	5c
75.	Toy	6m	E1	5c
76.	L'Horla	9m	E1	5b
77.	Edler Crack	20m	E2	5b
78.	Canoe	6m	E1	5c
79.	Finger Distance	8m	E3	6b
80.	Kayak	8m	E1	5c
81.	Kappelout Direct	6m	E3	6b
82.	Vain	15m	E2	5b
83.	Colossus	11m	E1	5b
84.	Saddy	10m	E1	5b
85.	Smoke Ont'Water	9m	E1	5c
86.	Squint	9m	E1	5b
87.	Fidget	7m	E1	6a
88.	Afterbirth	6m	E2	5c
89.	Birthday Groove	6m	E1	5c
90.	Diet of Worms	7m	E3	5b
91.	Dead Bay Groove	11m	E1	5b
92.	Dead Bay Crack	11m	E1	5b
93.	Black Nix Wall	7m	E1	5c
94.	Rat Scabies	11m	E3	6c
95.	Mister Softee	12m	E2	5c
96.	Apollo	16m	E2	6b
97.	Soyuz	10m	E2	5c
98.	A.P. Jacket	10m	E3	5c
99.	Unreachable Star	7m	E2	6a
100.	Ulysses or Bust	8m	E5	6b

Technique: Slabs

WHEN A SLAB IS A SLAB

Rock features shade into one another, especially at the hard grades, and become resistant to definition. On a relatively featureless limestone cliff, for instance, you may spend some time searching for an arête which turns out in the end to be more of a rib. As you shuffle about in the wild garlic and the old chalk-block wrappers at the bottom, staring irritably upwards, it occurs to you that the description 'arête' is an effect of scale, or of contrast with other nearby features. Elsewhere you find yourself wondering why the slab you're on looks more like a wall.

In 1965, Alan Blackshaw was able to describe a slab authoritatively, as a feature with something between thirty and sixty degrees of tilt; by now, slabs seem to have become fifteen degrees steeper, and in 1987 we would set the upper limit nearer seventy-five. But that's only half the story. A slab is not just a feature – it is an invitation to certain *types* of climbing, the geological cue which prompts you to use a certain section of your technical vocabulary. 'Slabbiness' is thus equally determined by the kind of rock you are on. Friction climbing on a fifty-degree slab of glacier-polished granite is going to be harder than on Derbyshire gritstone at the same angle. By the same token a rough slab doesn't get hard until it's at a much steeper angle than a smooth one, so it's common to come across quite vertical 'slabs', especially on low, one-pitch crags in Great Britain.

This approach enables us to divide slabs into two broad categories. On one hand, the slate you find in places like Dinorwic Quarry, the polished granite of the Handegg Walls or Yosemite, limestone (though there aren't many limestone slabs as such), the low friction rocks; and on the other hand the high friction rocks like gritstone, southern sandstone, and the rougher granites and gabbros. On a low-friction rock you will be looking for well-defined holds, however small they are. They aren't so important on high-friction rock, but that isn't to say you can pass them up.

Slate, with its laminar, easily split structure, tends to a surface of tiny, flaky, but distinct holds and hairline cracks. Gritstone is often studded with quartz pebbles the local lads call 'crystal', which are allowing the concept 'slab' to be pushed vertically towards meaninglessness. Sandstone suffers periodic erosion into weird useful dimples and soft pockets (you find the latter on gritstone too, where they can be scruffier and a lot more friable, a bit of the seaside at Millstone Edge).

If you find holds, you edge. If not, you smear. Both

Gill Fawcett on *Comes the Dervish* E3 5c Llanberis.

techniques require good balance. Both require you to think with your feet.

From the ridiculous to the sublime

There's a classic photograph of an early ascent of *Grey Slab*, Glydr Fawr, which shows the climber standing bolt upright in a tweed coat, tips of the fingers just touching rock, in a copybook illustration of the style of the day. (Authorizing this style forty years later, Blackshaw says that slabs promote 'a good climbing position. It is usually possible to rest at frequent intervals'.) He's smoking a pipe. In those days they had all the time in the world. A modern slab climb is going to be a little more demanding – not so static, at best a cross between a chess problem and a ballet, at worst a serious competition between movement and gravity. But that old picture does say something useful, which is that because you climb slabs with your feet, boots are important.

Get a pair that fit, particularly across the broad part of your foot. The tighter you can get them there the less lateral torsion there will be when you put your weight on the slab. Nothing reduces your accuracy with slab holds, or makes you feel insecure on them, more than a boot that twists round on your foot. All boots stretch, even if they're advertised as constructed not to, so buy them a bit too tight to allow for that. Don't bother with the salesman who tells you an extra pair of socks stuffed in will do the job. It won't. That's in the past with *Grey Slab* on Glydr Fawr. To be honest, I buy my boots very tight indeed. I put them on with a shoe-horn and they hurt all day. It would alarm a chiropodist but it assures real one-to-one contact with the rock.

After you've been climbing for a while, especially on a cool day, you may want to stop and tighten your laces. A good way of shrinking a suede upper that has stretched from use is to chuck it in the bath for a couple of hours. Remember to put some water in too.

Climbing on marginal adhesion makes you feel-good, but make sure you've chosen the adventure. Check the critical wear-areas round the toe of the boot for tell-tale white patches: these are nature's way of telling you your rubber has worn out. Most people favour one foot, so the wear will show up on that boot first.

It's haphazard, too, to climb in muddy boots. Always try to carry a towel (I like mine labelled 'Tetleys'): why climb on mud, sheep turds or vegetable juice when you've paid seventy pounds for butyl?

Shock Horror Slab, E1 6b, Stanage Edge.

OUT ON THE EDGE

A high step is a typical move on slate, Britain's premier edging rock, and it can go like this:

Above you on the slab there are two little incuts, one higher than the other, more or less well-spaced. Your aim is to be standing on the lower one. The closer they are together vertically, and the further apart horizontally, the harder the move will be.

To get into position, crimp your fingers over the higher hold and run your feet up the slab. The higher they come in this phase the better, because this will push your body outwards and away from the slab. In a high slab your knee has to tuck in somewhere, or it will push you off. You could, if circumstances encourage it, face slightly to one side or the other, so that your knee can move sideways a little, giving it more room.

Once you've cranked your foot as high as possible and the edge of your boot is on the foothold, remember to move your body back in, otherwise you won't transfer your weight efficiently. At the same time as you are moving back in, you will need to be making fairly violent use of the handhold, first pulling on it like mad, and then, as soon as you're high enough, pushing down. The more height you can gain like this, the easier it will be to complete the move by rocking your weight

fully onto the foothold. After that, stand up for a mantelshelf. (You may find yourself extending your fingers until they're pointing straight down onto the handhold, to gain extra height.)

Like any move, this will be part of a sequence – it has evolved out of the move before, and as you leave it, it is shading irretrievably into the next one – and it's done dynamically. You often have to throw yourself into, or through, moves like these. That isn't possible except on a positive hold: similar moves in smearing country mustn't be done explosively because your foot will simply shoot off the slab.

Using the edge of the boot is easier if it has a stiffened sole. Some manufacturers, like Kamet, produce a boot designed for edging. 'Disco dazzlers', flexibly constructed and cut low in the ankle are best saved for après-climb situations, or at any rate for smearing. Clearly, an edging boot should have a nice sharp edge on it: you are going to be standing on some very small holds indeed. Keeping an edge is not so easy since the demise of hard rubber. When you edge, the rand of the boot is in contact with the rock, so Boreal have produced a Firé with a sticky rand to counteract rolling. Otherwise, you might twist your boot fractionally into the hold to stop it rolling off. In the end all you can do is

Edging on *Downhill Racer* E4 6a, Froggatt Edge.

Squeaking the boot.

make sure plenty of bodyweight is going on to the hold. Edging holds are positive, and you have to accept and exploit that, however microscopic they seem.

Framing rules for the way you present your boot to the rock illustrates the difficulty of making generalizations about modern hard climbing. It's all very well to say that edging is best done with the heel of the boot lower than the ball of the foot, but this becomes meaningless when the angle of the foot-hold means it can only be used toe-down. Because every edging hold is at a different angle, and because every crucial arrangement of holds is different from every other, rules of thumb will only get in your way. In the end, you do what the rock compels you to.

Flexibility is the only rule. Whether you face left or right, use the inner or outer edge of the boot, be aware of what will best keep you in balance and moving fluidly into the next part of the sequence. There's no 'only' way to solve a problem if you do plenty of bouldering to extend your technical vocabulary, and then use your imagination.

The smear test

The psychology of edging is the psychology of stress: but there's no stress like the concentration and delicacy needed when you smear a big, open, unprotected slab. Smearing is one of the major tests of nerve.

It originated as a technique with Pierre Alain and the first friction boot, designed for the sandstone boulders at Fontainebleau in the nineteen thirties, and in Britain it was carried to the extremes that old-fashioned 'hard' rubber can achieve by the gritstone slab climbers of the middle seventies. With the appearance of butyl rubber compounds and the Boreal Firé, it grew wings. High-friction boot and high-friction rock have come together on crags like the Roaches in Staffordshire to produce high anxiety climbing.

To smear, you play off the angle of the slab against its coefficient of friction. This demands a clean boot. Butyl is beautiful but it isn't infallible. It has chemical and design limits. If the pores in the rubber become clogged, it won't stick so well. Washing the sole after use can guard against a long-term build-up of dirt. In the short-term – i.e. before you set out on the route – take any obvious dirt off with your towel, then squeak the boot. You can do this with spit and your thumb, rubbing till the rubber squeaks; or with methylated spirit on a cloth. The whole sole might as well be clean, but obviously the most important area is forward of the instep, around the ball of the foot.

(There is one other way to improve the adhesion of butyl rubbers. But I would never recommend warming the boot gently with a blowlamp to the nervous, the careless or those of a highly ethical disposition. . .)

100% smearing: an arête at Caley Crag.

Now you're sure your pores aren't clogged up, next thing is to clean the house. Avoid outdoor pursuits groups, who often appropriate steep slabs in the name of abseil practice, trampling down them in muddy trainers and walking boots. A wet slab is no use to anyone – wait for a light drying wind, a nice sunny day. In summer there might be dust or sand underfoot. The former will clog your pores, the latter will slide about like ball bearings (or embed itself in the rubber, destroying the surface). Dried-up lichen can be a nuisance.

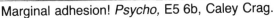

Marginal adhesion! *Psycho,* E5 6b, Caley Crag.

Stubborn lichen is easily sorted out with a wire brush by abseil, but be careful not to overdo it. Make sure the difficulty of the climb warrants this sort of treatment and that the rock is hard enough to stand it – under the brush, sandstone melts away before your eyes. (Brushing goes unpredictably in and out of fashion, especially if you aren't a local climber and in the know. In some enclaves, wire-brushing and hold-improvement are held to be inseparable concepts. People have a right to be touchy about it: hold-improvement and even outright chipping are endemic these days, especially in bouldering spots.)

For cleaning as you go, a toothbrush would seem reasonable; or you can use your towel. If the slab is anything like hard, cleaning as you climb may require more hands than you are supplied with.

Edging moves are designer moves, sharp, tight and aggressive. Smearing is more of an inner game, fluid,

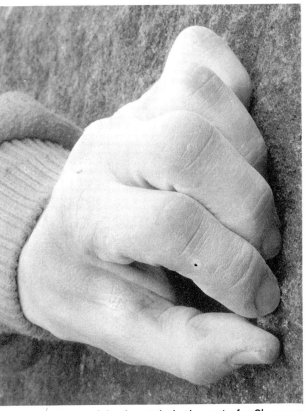

Top and above: A horizontal pinch, part of a 6b move on *Daydreamer*, Stanage Edge.

instinctive. The kinds of moves you do on smeared slabs are high steps, long reaches, infinitely delicate mantelshelves. You must move confidently but not too fast. Balance becomes desperately important, controlling the careful shift of weight from hold to hold.

It's important to remember to keep moving on a slab, especially on smears. Once you stop, starting up again begins to look more and more impossible. Let the moves evolve smoothly out of one another, propelled by both physical and psychological momentum.

To get help with the smear, look for slight indentations and dimples in the rock; look for flatter patches, and patches of rougher or cleaner rock. Even someone else's rubber marks can provide a clue (often an equivocal one: he tried it, but that doesn't mean it worked!) The whole science of friction is to keep as much rubber on the rock as possible. Be aware of angles. Look for new ways to get your sole flat on the rock. Use your ankle imaginatively, as a kind of ball-joint. Everything I've said about lateral torsion applies to smearing: friction is powered by energy. You can't allow the energy of your bodyweight to be diverted into twisting the boot round your foot. On a really hard slab, that instant of leakage may occur in the only time you have to use the hold successfully. Great amounts of psychic energy are necessary to climb slabs – don't waste it feeling insecure about your boots.

Tuck the ends of your laces out of the way.

Hands on your slab, or: the pebble dash

Outside a mantel or palming-down movement, hands can feel a bit vestigial on the easier-angled slab. This is an illusion. Like an insect trying not to break the surface tension of water, you must always be spreading and lifting your weight. The pads of your fingers, held almost flat against the rock, can make a (strenuous) push-down hold out of a slight change in angle. There are often little vertical features that can be exploited as layaways or sidepulls; they may be shallow and rounded but they are an armoury of ways to stay in balance. And on steep gritstone slabs there are pebbles.

Pebbles can be used to back up a smear in the same way as any other small positive hold, allowing you to run your feet up the slab; or they can be climbed as an end in themselves. Use them for one- or two-finger pulls, with your thumb folded over your fingernail to lock your fingers on. Pinchgrip them. Look for smooth-topped or flat-topped pebbles, pebbles with side incut.

Watch the thin ones, and the ones that stick out a long way. They may snap off. 'Outdoor pursuits', having muddied your slab, can strip it of a crucial pebble too, making it more difficult (or even impossible). Sharp pebbles can shred your fingertips, especially if you are

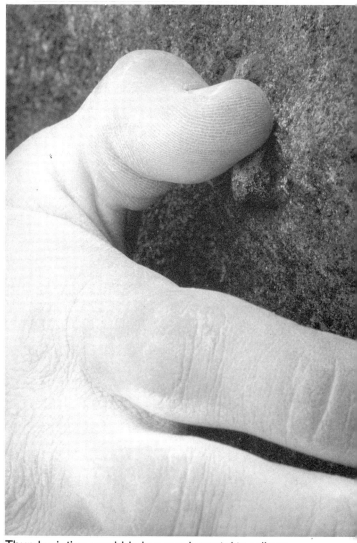

Thumbprinting a pebble in a semi-mantel to relieve sore fingers!

repeating one move over and over again as in a boulder problem, to the point where you can't climb again until they've healed. Limit the damage by reversing the procedure described above, and hook your thumb over the pebble first, clamping your fingers down on top of it. This can make quite a satisfactory hold – and your thumb isn't as vital to you as your fingertips!

Chains of pebbles demand cunning. Starting out on the wrong edge can wrong-foot you further, leading to multiplying errors and a nightmare of lost balance, wrong-handing and bad decisions, where every move is an attempt to correct the consequences of the last. Sequences of moves need to be thought out carefully before you commit yourself to a slab; or even practised beforehand.

The friction of pebbles isn't anywhere near as high as

the rock they are embedded in, so be careful. Feel for surface rugosities and deformities.

The mantelshelf is a common move on slabs. On a smearing slab perhaps the most difficult phase of the mantelshelf is the push–down. A slight bulge in the surface will allow you to use the heel of your palm for this, or the side of it below the little finger. Otherwise, the whole palm goes onto the rock, fingers pointing down. Don't forget to chalk the part of your hand in use; but don't forget that chalk decreases friction for boots, so if you're planning to use the same hold for both hand and foot, chalk up as lightly as possible. (The boulderers at Fontainebleau use very small, 'fingertip' chalkbags, and rub the chalk well in so as little as possible is transferred to the rock.)

1. A right-hand layaway holds the body into the slab; feet on friction enabling . . .

2. transfer of weight to the left palm. *Throw* yourself into it. By now both feet are on friction. . .

Left: Extreme palming on a boulder problem at Caley, Yorkshire.

3. A pull on the pebble allows the climber to pivot on left wrist and bring right foot . . .

4. up onto the mantelhold. From here stand up very carefully indeed: don't stand on your hand!

In general

Don't get lost, especially when smearing. Keep a lively eye open for holds, and an open mind on what a hold can be. All the 'don'ts' of the past (don't do high steps or long reaches, they throw you out of balance, etc., etc.,) are out the window now, and 'good style' is authorized by the route itself.

A hard slab lead is likely to be a solo, even at the lower extreme grades.

At the beginning look for slabs that can be protected with a side-runner. A long pendulum can be a nose-grinder but it has the advantage that it allows you to go on living after your first mistake.

On slate, the higher extreme grades tend to be bolted for protection, but you confront the gritstone horrors without any help at all, so it's wise to top-rope first. Check that the local ethic encourages this. If you practise on a top-rope moves that are commonly done – or were done originally – on sight, you are cheating.

Half of what makes a slab climb 'modern' is its intensity, that is, its technical difficulty. This makes it unlikely that you will find a nice 5 cm ledge to rest on halfway up. Your brain gets tired of working out the sequences, stringing combinations together like a world-class chess player; your calves just get tired. Rest where and how you can, transferring your weight to any positive handhold: otherwise it's just a matter of shifting position, flexing your leg, changing feet. On a really demanding slab nothing like this will turn up, and that is why training is important.

Psychological training is synonymous with experience. To handle the high exposure and head-stress of slab climbing, climb more slabs. To improve the strength and stamina of your calves, place a batten of wood 60 × 5 × 4 cm on the floor of the gym, and with a weight across your shoulders, use it like a step: start with the ball of your foot on it and your heel on the floor, then stretch up on your toes and – slowly – back down again. A killer! At home – training on the cheap – fill a rucksack with all your discarded Hexentric 11s and use it instead of a barbell. Suppleness of the legs and hips can be increased by ballet- or yoga-based stretching exercises (see training section.)

A long way up on *Black Wall Eliminate*, Almscliffe.

Technique: Walls

'Walls,' Alan Blackshaw felt able to state authoritatively in 1965, 'are between 60 and 90 degrees.' By 1987 they have become a bit steeper, indeed many of them overhang insistently, and because of this what remains relevant in Blackshaw's definitions is not the topography but the caution that follows on its heels: 'The steeper the wall, the more important it is to climb it properly, because you will tire quickly and become unsafe. *You must plot your moves ahead . . . so they you can maintain rhythm and balance. . .*'. The italics in this recipe for hyper-modern wall-climbing are mine.

Walls are often a race against failing strength. They are as exposed as slabs. A bit unnerved by this the earlier climbers clung to the gullies and sunny ridges. They preferred a well-defined route anyway. But in the end

Necronomicon, Verdon Gorge.

that was the exact challenge the walls represented. You might go anywhere on them. Like any new territory they were so full of possibility they induced a kind of vertigo. By the end of the nineteenth century this had proved too attractive to resist: climbers like Owen Glynne Jones and William Slingsby had launched themselves into the big open space.

(They had their moral doubts still. Were the walls a 'justifiable' place to climb? Should they record their routes, for fear of encouraging others? O. G. Jones worked out with weights in Kensington but refused to recommend the Solly/Slingsby creation of 1892, *Eagles Nest Ridge Direct*.)

Since then the antithesis has been constantly restated – periods of comfortable 'feature' climbing precede sudden unreasoning lurches out onto the walls.

The latest wave of colonization got its impetus in 1974 from Peter Livesey's lead of *Right Wall*, Dinas Cromlech, at E5 6a. Livesey had already done technically harder things on limestone, and later the same year he was to produce *Footless Crow*, also E5 6a, on Goat Crag, probably the most achieved wall climb of its day: but *Right Wall* was the breakthrough. It listed the possibilities. It was scary, strenuous, exposed and sustained; and at that time you had to go for the crux section with only a thin tape and a few shaky wires for protection. I made the second ascent with Chris Gibb.

Right Wall signalled a rush of development by local climbers in the Lakes, the Peak, the south. Meanwhile adrenalin and ambition took Livesey and me all over the country.

Everything was up for grabs. We would drive down to Cornwall for a day on a rumour. *Liberator*, E4 6a, came about because we'd read an article by Pat Littlejohn on the remaining aid-points in the Great Zawn, Bosigran. It was a gnarly day, all wet and green, with a grey sea slapping the bottom of the cliff. Trying to use a pinchgrip to lean left, Pete dislocated his shoulder and fell off. He must have been in pain but by then our relationship was a competitive one, and he was determined to lead the pitch. His shoulder came out again on the same move, so eventually we swapped over. I led the pitch, but I might as well have soloed it. There were no belay-brakes in those days, so Pete wrapped the rope a couple of times round his good arm. . . .

Protection was improving by 1979 when I took the *Right Wall* philosophy a little further and added *Lord of the Flies*, E6 6a, to Dinas Cromlech: though I still had only one runner in the last 18 metres. (There is TV footage of the first ascent. In the upper section of the wall, my hair is 20 cm longer than in the lower. This isn't because the climb took months, but because we had only one camera, and Sid Perou ran out of film while I was still involved with the top wall. He was so appalled by the climb that to keep me calm he pretended to go on filming! We went back later to do the bits he'd missed.)

By 1981 I was using pre-placed bolt protection to push the walls. If bolts were to be accepted by British climbers I knew they would have to be 'sportingly' placed. Perhaps at the beginning I overdid it. On *Tequila Mockingbird* at Chee Tor I arranged things so that the first 7 metres were unprotected: a friend of mine promptly fell off and broke his wrists. I felt guilty about that but there's no doubt that it lessened the ethical impact of the bolts.

This was the beginning of the blank wall revolution, which led inevitably to the Europeanization of radically steep cliffs like Raven Tor, Derbyshire; and to state-of-the-art climbs like *Revelations*.

FEET

Walls are steep: get as much of your weight on your feet as possible. I try to keep my feet in contact even when there aren't any holds. The slightest bit of friction will take some weight off your arms. Look for tiny indents and bulges – often on limestone the only way you know it's a hold is by the smear of rubber.

Boots are obviously vital to this transaction. Don't go onto pockety limestone in a round-toed boot; equally, make sure your toes are pushed well down into a pointy toe, otherwise you might as well climb in clowns' shoes. For tiny incuts the boot needs a good edge, but not too good: a new edge is so sharp it may flex and pop off a small hold! Whether on pockets or incuts, using the toe-edge of your boot is like front-pointing with a crampon, so you want the boot tight to stiffen your foot. Remember that you can turn your foot and use the heel too. This is especially good for a rest.

When abandoning a trusty foothold, leave your foot in place for as long as possible so that you're operating from a secure base. At the same time remember that lifting your heel from the horizontal will bring the rand of your boot in contact with vertical or past-vertical rock: if you are standing on a small edge, this may push your foot off. Any kind of movement is bad footwork on small holds. Put your foot on and keep it there.

On steep or overhanging rock it's hard to see what your feet are doing. Either develop your instincts by constant bouldering, or try and memorize a possible foothold while it's still at eye-level; if you mark it with chalk, mark *above*. Too obvious a foot-placement deserves suspicion – it may start you on a false sequence, with a resulting loss of upward momentum. Your best pocket hold is slightly recessed in its top lip; otherwise squash the butyl into whatever's there, wriggling your toe to seat it in the pocket. (Progress has been reported

With the right boot you can stand on a pocket this small.

here with the flexible 'rock slipper' – you can actually get a big-toe in a pocket with these if you can stand the agony!)

It's so easy to swing out of balance on a wall, and the foot-hook is an ideal way to combat this. But its primary use is as a hold. If, for instance, you have a reasonable right foothold, and a good handhold in line, a left foot-hook will enable you to reach up with your left hand. The bluntest arête feature or bulge can give opportunities for this technique. New, sticky-randed boots encourage you to use the side of your foot for it.

Opposite: Masters of the Modern Dance: high-stepping it on a problem at Rheinstor, Derbyshire.

Above: *Pebble Mill*, E4 6b, Burbage South.

THE NUMBERS

High grade climbing is an aesthetic, almost an intellec-
tual experience of your own movement. It organizes
that emotional mixture you feel at the lower grades –
adrenalin buzz, kinaesthesia, the satisfaction of correct-
ly applying a correct solution under stress – and concen-
trates it. All the old virtues of danger and excitement are
present, but they are disciplined by a debilitating
technicality.

Climbing Johnny Dawes's direct start to *Living at the
Speed* 6c, Stanage Edge.

2. Horizontal jams: smear with the feet until . .

1. Don't step on the snow.

4. The ripple is only good in two places: with fingers locked on, work left foot as high as possible, to allow right foot to step over the overlap . . .

3. you can get into balance to reach up with right hand for the thin ripple above. Note how the climber leans *away* from left hand.

Modern routes are extended boulder problems. At 6c and 7a you don't use smaller holds as such; you only marshall more of them, into more intricate sequences. These sequences, which are like codes, or musical notation, are the grammar that binds the individual 'words' (moves) of the 'sentence' (climb) together. They are called The Numbers.

You learn the *general* rules of combination by climbing on as many different crags and types of rock as you can. Your most precious piece of equipment is your software, your vocabulary of movements. Nurture it. It must be constantly renewed. Every time you solve a boulder problem you are adding a new 'word' to it, a new way of attaching one step to another.

6. into a finger-straining mantel . . .

5. . . . looking for the next move as you turn fingerholds into mantels. Right foot on a poor smear, left foot nowhere, begin to push up . . .

8. Two pebble-holds make it easier to transfer weight to poor left foothold, then step up with the right. Go for the break!

7. poor left foot smears back up the right foot, as you reach for a pebble – weight still on left hand.

Traditionally the rules that govern a *particular* route are learned while you are climbing it. This was possible only when climbs gave you time to think. (Climbs like this still exist, of course, in their thousands: and you will make no new friends if you top-rope or hangdog their 5 cm resting ledges and easily-reversible moves into submission. We are not talking about them.) But this simply won't do for a modern wall climb. From the first move you are in a race between gravity and strength, across sequences so complex they may have taken months to assemble, and which just cannot be retrieved by a traditional 'on sight' leader before he falls off.

Pocket climbing at Rheinstor, Britain's 'Little Buoux' (very little).

2. vicious pull on left middle finger; to maintain balance allow right leg to swing through. This cuts out a foot-change, so that . . .

1. Weight on right hand in pocket (one finger, middle); toes in good pockets; left hand middle finger pocket . . .

4. Left foot comes up into toe-tip pocket. Because this cranks you over slightly to the left . . .

3. you can step straight up with right foot, while reaching fast for a two-finger pocket.

To get up climbs like these you must learn, and then be obsessed by, The Numbers. At night when I close my eyes I can see the enchained steps of a hundred different hard climbs. My nightmare is of a sequence blown and breaking up from some multiplying error. You knew what to do but you thought you'd try something different, and now the whole structure is going down like a line of dominoes.

When the magic works, each move is chained to or evolves out of the last, to construct the single entrancing super-move which is the pitch. Static climbing is no longer appropriate. Within a square metre you will exploit four or five tiny, individually useless, holds, shifting between them controlledly until they make one good one, all the time falling in and out of balance, directing little swings and barndoors – almost as if, rather than initiating it, you are editing movement that is already there. Climbing never was a matter of maintaining your position anyway, but of moving on. This foothold won't support you? Turn it into an opposition-hold for a fraction of a second then say goodbye to it forever. Don't think you can be a wall-flower, you came here to dance.

6. Weight swings back onto right foot, enabling the high step. Pull like mad on left hand – a real shoulder-dislocator.

5. make sure left foot shares the weight to balance you as you reach for the next hold – two fingers *vertically* stacked in the left pocket.

8. Pull until left leg straight; jump-change to right foot; left leg out – boot rand friction – to maintain balance.

7. Keep pulling and slap for the tiny layaway with your right hand. Straight leg, with tip of toe just brushing rock, holds you in balance.

HANDS

The important thing with a small edge is to get as many fingers round it as possible. One finger is strenuous and unstable, two fingers much firmer, and if you can crook your thumb over them to form a solid unit, so much the better. Three fingers are solid. Try to find room for your little finger as well – it won't contribute much but it will make the hold feel very stable indeed because all the forearm muscles will be in play. You can stack fingers on some small holds almost as you would in a flared peg socket: three fingers always make a stronger unit than two. Put the index and ring fingers on the hold, then press down on them with the middle finger.

Half the disadvantage of a very small hold is that energy must be wasted keeping the fingers in place on it. Crimp your fingers on, never pull outwards. Arrange your wrist and arm to direct your effort downwards. Friction is as important to a fingerhold as to a foothold, particularly on limestone, where you might have only a sloping dimple to work with. Chalk up. A small undercut can be stabilized by pinching it: that is, by using the overlap as a kind of rim. This also allows you to push down a little against your thumb.

Pinchgripping is as basic a technique to modern wall-climbing as the heel-hook. Limestone pinches tend to be stalactites or flowstones, standing out from the wall in such a way as to make a flange you can get your hand or fingers round. Because you can pull sideways and outwards on it, a pinchgrip makes a useful if tiring one-hold unit. The distinction between pinchgrip and lay-away soon blurs. If it's a long way to the side of you, a small pinch is used as a side pull; but as soon as it's directly in front you are forced into a pure pinch, using only the muscles of your forearm to clamp your hand onto the hold. Obviously this is tiring and to be avoided. The problem with pinchgrips is often to stop your fingers sliding down them. Pinchgripping without a flange is like pulling up on a roof-beam – hard. Look for irregularities or ripples; and again, layaway from them if you can. This will bring your bodyweight to the rescue of your abused forearm.

Pocket-climbing is common in Europe, where at crags like Buoux it has been brought to an art. The pocket is the ultimate one-hold unit – you can pull up on its bottom lip, side-pull, then undercling the top lip. The deeper the pocket the more stable a hold it makes. Try and get your fingers in up to the second joint, especially in one-finger placements. (Deep one-finger pockets can be frightening. What if your digit stays behind when you fall off? This is less of a danger than it first seems.) A shallow one-finger placement is almost like inserting a crampon point into the rock – make it rigid by locking your thumb over the top, as you would with a small incut.

Look for the best lip on the pocket. By arranging your fingers as for a side-pull you may still get excellent downward pull, so don't be literalistic. (Adjust your fingers in the pocket anyway, for best use. You may have to tip them over slightly, especially if you are going to move smoothly into a side-pull.) Equally don't limit yourself, in a two-finger placement, to index and middle. Pocket climbing is sensuous climbing. Feel out the internal geography of the pocket to see if more efficient use could be made by, say, index and ring fingers – some pockets may have to be used with the fingers slightly separated: strenuous and painful! – or by a stack of three fingers against a lip or inner irregularity. You can exploit a good pocket to waist height or higher. It will also hold you into the rock and redirect your weight onto your feet.

Sharp pockets hurt. (In France some are permanently taped. Taping your fingers to protect them is less efficient.)

Always close your unused fingers into a little fist, and keep your wrist against the wall: this not only acts as a clamp to stabilize the hold, it also supports your arched fingers, taking some of the strain off the tendons. Pocket country is unsympathetic to finger tendons.

1. Use the whole of a hold even though part of it isn't so good.

2. Use of a one-finger pocket.

3. Using a small pinchgrip.

Using an undercut.

RESTING

On a modern wall it's important to rest whenever the opportunity presents itself. You may feel strong now, but later you won't and by then the route will have withdrawn its sympathy.

We've already established that climbing – especially on steep ground – is no longer a static discipline. ('Generally,' Alan Blackshaw reminds us hollowly from the Department of Trade and Industry in 1965, 'it does not pay to hang about on walls.' Was he speaking figuratively or literally?) At the hard grades resting is hardly a static process any more either. There will be chances to rest one limb or part of it, but not much else. If you have been doing a lot of 'front pointing' in pockets, for example, turn your foot and get your heel on a hold. This will ease not only the foot but the ankle and the calf muscle too, by directing your weight straight down through the bones of your leg. Similarly, rest your arms by deadhanging.

Either of these mechanisms will allow you to disengage one limb and shake it out; as will the use of a horizontal break for heel- or foot-hooking. With a foot in the break you can take one hand out. The circulation of the blood is as vulnerable to gravity as you are.

Modern wall climbing demands that your hands be above your head a disproportionate amount of the time. You can't obey the old rule and keep your hands low. At the exact point when overworked muscles demand more oxygen, it thus becomes harder for the heart to supply. Shake-outs aren't twenty minutes in the cafe with a bun, but they will help.

Just as you can use a heel to rest, don't forget that you can swap to an outside edge. Laying away with the right hand, for instance, you might place the outside edge of the left boot so that you can pull yourself in over it and shake out your left hand. Keep your weight on your feet whenever you may, and look for balance through gravity.

In the end though, resting is an occasional pastime. Modern climbs don't encourage it, and a significant number of them won't allow it at all. At E6 and 7 you must simply climb the route as fast as possible. Your only rest will be at the top. Train for stamina. Learn the route so you don't waste effort. I never go for a hard climb at the end of a tiring day, but instead spend a day rehearsing the moves; rest that evening and all the next day; then go back to it the following evening when the air is cool and the signs good. Rather than rest on a route like this, be rested when you start.

Opposite page: *Cave Route Left Hand* E6 6c, Gordale, Yorkshire.

Above: Using a heel-hook to rest on the first ascent of *King Swing* E6 6b, Malham, Yorkshire.

FALLING

In Europe you will climb with bolt protection. You cannot ignore the possibility that you will fall off. In a way, if you aren't falling you aren't learning. This is a radical way of putting it, I know. 'The leader never falls,' they used to insist. But we don't live in 1887 any more. Why feel we have to climb there?

Zoolook, E7 6c, at Malham Cove, is less a wall than a continuous overhang. When I came to make the first lead of it, I found it hard to prepare: some of the bolts were well placed but the rest had to go wherever I could manage to put them. As a result some of them involve very long reaches and bizarre clips. Two thirds of the way up, *Zoolook* becomes more of a flight than a climb, abandoning not only the rules the Victorian climber climbed by, but any rules he could imagine. Bootstrapping up through serial overhangs by slapping at the wall – slap from the layaway: feet up: slap from the layaway: the climber is more off than on the rock. Positive holds are a memory. Half-way through this blitz, he must clip one of the most difficult bolts of the lot.

From an abseil rope I was using to clean another climb I watched young Sheffield climber Ben Moon

A fall from *King Swing* maroons you in the middle of nowhere!

attempt the second ascent. He'd done the first hard section beautifully, passed the roof, and now entered the layaways, climbing in Lycra tights and a knackered T shirt. He knew this was the crucial clip. He had one end of a quickdraw already krabbed onto the rope, so only one movement was necessary to get it off the harness and though the bolt-hanger.

Unfortunately he forgot to tell Mark, who was belaying, about his plan. He ripped the quickdraw off – not enough rope to clip! – flopped back onto the layaways somehow, pumped and cursing and trying to remember how far down the last bolt was.

'Come on Ben!'

It was slipping away from him. He grabbed the quickdraw, lurched for the bolt, forgot a second time to ask for slack. . .

'Come on Ben!'

Back on the layaways, shaking with total body-pump, terminal pump, knowing that he'd lost his chance, he shouted, 'Give us loads of slack!' and fell over backwards. As he fell he got hold of the quickdraw in both hands and slammed it at the bolt-hanger. For a millisecond I thought it had gone home – I heard the krab hit the bolt-head, *click* – and then it was goodbye. I had been hardly three metres from him thoughout, talking, looking into his eyes as he tottered. All I had time to say now was, 'Oh Ben. Oh no,' as the krab banged off the bolt and with a wail Ben shot away, his dreadlocks flying and his arms waving.

He was climbing on single 8½ mm rope, to save weight. Before it stopped him he had fallen fifteen metres like a puppet on a bit of elastic.

All you can do about the psychological effects of falling is get used to them. This is as true of an unprotected fall from a boulder-problem – where the risk of damage is a little higher – but not, clearly, of a fall when soloing. . . .

You can limit the immediate physical consequences of a 'safe' fall by bearing some things in mind. The most obvious point is: choose where you fall. Modern wall climbs by definition (bolted or protected by traditional methods) are likely to be on very steep or overhanging rock. This makes it less likely that you will bump into something while you are falling (this can't be said of a VS). Even so, try not to fall too close to the wall. A small ledge will break your ankle if you catch it with your foot on the way down. Similarly, remember how easy it is to swing back under an overhang; and watch out for the pendulum that ends up in a corner – in this case the term 'safe' might mean 'some concussion and two broken ribs'.

The second point is: try to choose *how* you fall. Get your feet away from the rock before your hands, or at least at the same time. It's worthwhile making a conscious effort over this, to avoid falling upside down. Don't turn outwards as you would instinctively from a bouldering fall. You aren't looking for a landing place, and in a modern harness you are better facing the rock. If you want something to do with your hands, hold the rope near the knot. It will then be located properly relative to the harness. It will be out of the way, too – if you fall with the rope between your legs and behind your thighs you can come in for rope burns and some other nasty damage. And be careful not to ladder your tights.

To conquer the natural fear of falling takes practice. The only problem with this is the wear and tear on your equipment. A common method of fall-training is to place a good solid runner by abseil, top-rope up to it, then 'lead' above it, jumping off first from waist level, then foot level, then with your feet a metre above the runner – and so on, until you have begun to accept quite big falls. But every one of them is taking some life out of your rope, and in this instance the runner too. (*Don't* use an old rope to 'save' on your good ones – this is to court serious injury.) I prefer to do my falling on routes: go for it, and instead of going through that period of grip and desperation when things don't work out, simply jump off. This has the advantage of teaching you how to be in control of your falls in a real situation.

Falling off, deliberately or otherwise, comes with a government health warning. Do be careful how you place your protection. Be intelligent about commonly-used runner-placements on popular routes: how many hundreds of falls have they now taken? In the Peak District, commonly used runner placements are beginning to explode, the rock has become so weakened. This has happened recently on *Landsickness*, E3 6a, on Gardoms Edge, and on *Deadbay Groove*, E3 6a, at Curbar (the same unlucky leader involved in both cases!) Neither should you assume that all bolts are bombproof. . . .

British climbs, especially long-established climbs and climbs on sea-cliffs, where there is a spectacular acceleration of all the normal erosion processes, are now studded with eroded pegs, loose and rusty bolts, and bits of tat degraded by ultra-violet exposure. By this they are rendered a good deal less 'safe' than the opponents of modern climbing believe! So check them. Attempts are being made by the BMC to decide a bolt-replacement policy. But the climbing community, always aware of the erosions of freedom necessitated by official action, are undecided as to how and who; and it's recently become clear that if the BMC took over this duty it would become legally liable under the Health and Safety at Work Act for the individual climber's safety on a bolted cliff. This would put them in the ludicrous position of any quarry owner.

BOLT PLACEMENT AND CLIPPING

The chief difficulty in preparing *Zoo Look* was that it had never been aided. There were no old bolts or *in situ* pegs which would allow you to swing in on your abseil rope and anchor yourself while you worked. Instead I had to grab a handhold each time, then place a skyhook in a pocket to keep me in position! Several days are often needed to prepare a climb like this one.

A star drill takes between ten and twenty minutes to make a hole for the standard 8 mm Rock anchor, the type in general use on modern British routes; longer for the 10 mm bolt which is replacing it because of its greater holding power. A Bosch drill is useful here! Clean out the hole, once you have made it, by blowing in it. Insert a little wedge. As you hammer it home the wedge expands and the anchor is fixed; you can unscrew the holder. Hangers come in several shapes and sizes, from companies like Petzl which manufacture caving equipment. (Caving magazines are useful sources of information on bolts and bolting.) They should be flush with the rock for maximum strength. Never overtighten a hanger: hand-tighten, then give no more than a three-quarter turn with a spanner.

Bolt hangers can unscrew themselves if you fall repeatedly to the left of them.

New systems like the German Buhler bolt rely on quick-setting cement. This is pumped into the hole and the bolt simply slid into it. These bolts have big-ringed hangers which are easier to clip, very strong indeed, and which won't unscrew. They can also be used for direct belays or lowering off, since they won't damage the rope.

The reliability of a bolt depends as much on the strength of the rock as the strength of the metal you put into it. Limestone, for instance, is often formed as a series of skins or shallow laminates, 'sheaves', the outer one of which is always ready to star-out like bad ice and shear off under load. In such a zone there might be only one patch of rock which will take a bolt. This not only means an awkward clip, or an over-sporting placement: it also means that the bolt can never be replaced, since it already occupies the only acceptable spot. (Because of this, 'safe' climbs are becoming inevitably less safe.)

Otherwise the difficulty of the clip – and the distance between clips – is decided by the climber who makes the route. There are two or three pitches on Raven Tor which bite as soon as you leave the ground: if you fall while you are clipping the second bolt on *Revelations*, E7 6c, and you are using a single rope, you will hit the ground. Routes are made things now, artefacts. Where is the line drawn between excitement and responsibility? Who draws it? These will be increasingly vexed questions. But we have a clear precedent, I think in the shape of the grading system itself, which requires that

Clipping a modern quickdraw.

someone draw a balance between danger and care every time a decision is made to up- or down-grade a climb.

To clip efficiently, rack your quickdraws according to a system. Take only as many as you need. You may have to learn the clips in the same way that you learn The Numbers. It helps to have at the bolt-end of the quickdraw a krab with a narrow nose – the hanger will accept it more easily; while at the rope-end you use a bent- or 'banana'-gated krab of a generous size, which will encourage the rope home. Practise with them. Many climbers are tempted to reach *up* for the clip, so that they feel safer sooner, and get some measure of overhead protection. This is not necessarily safe at all, and it's often better to wait until you are level with or even above a bolt before you clip – ease of clipping counts for a lot in energy-saving terms. Try to clip fluidly and (poor Ben's trials aside!) not to lunge for a bolt: it will unseat you. Watch out for the desperate Rotating Hanger, which spins coyly away from your karabiner every time you try to introduce it!

A typical bolted route at Malham.

TRAINING TIPS

Steep ground is a race against gravity. Technique and balance give you an edge, but in the end power and stamina will count heavily. The term 'rock athlete' gained currency as the new wall-climbs went up in the early to mid-seventies. This wasn't a coincidence. Wall climbers needed the explosive power of a sprinter or a shot-putter, the stamina of the middle distance runner.

Power pull-ups are the best exercise for the arms. Wolfgang Gulich, the top German climber, employs a device he designed himself. A pull-up bar is bolted over the top of his living room door, and from it hangs an elastic sling. As soon as he has exhausted his arms with ordinary pull-ups he puts one foot in this band, which takes some of his weight and thus enables him to pump even further. This Kafkaesque self-torture is not recommended for climbers new to training. Wolfgang looks like Muscle Beach. On the cheap, you can pull up from the door frame wearing your harness and a comprehensive rack of No 4 Friends.

A bit more expensive is a bolt-on fingerboard, which comes drilled with different sizes and depths of holes, for finger pull-ups. Be careful how you use these. They can be lethal on tendons, especially if you deadhang. I've always found commercial 'finger-exercisers' useless. You can squeeze them all day and they just seem to tire your forearms with no real result.

In steep limestone pocket climbing, you are front-pointing much of the time, rather than edging. The leverage on your calves is thus intense. Calf-raises, with weights, are the best exercise for this. You will also need to work your big thigh muscles. Flexibility exercises aid high steps and rock-overs. Top-roping on strenuous ground is good for stamina. But don't lower off: down-climb!

Strenuous climbing at Malham Cove.

Big roof on *Guadeloupe* E5 6b, Loup Scar, Yorkshire.

Technique: Overhangs

Eventually the wall forces you to admit it has become an overhang. It impends steadily, on a broad front. Or it might be interrupted piecemeal. Bulges – rounded, never toó extensive, always awkward because they suddenly change the rules on you – occur as features on walls; as do overlaps. It's size that distinguishes the overlap, like an inverted kerb, from the overhang proper: but I think a false size distinction is often made between overhang and roof. A roof is flattish and at a good angle to the wall underneath it – after that it can extend from two to a hundred and fifty metres. Stacked overhangs terminate the wall for good. Up there you are in a different kind of country, thinking your way through frontier after frontier.

In Britain the history of overhangs above the VS grade is the history of aid-climbing. Roofs – especially big ones – were a natural target for the peg, and lines of rusted stubs can still be seen in them, looking fibrous and natural like something that grows there. Great fun could be had in those days, out of the rain, swinging

1. A typical roof sequence just left of *Goblin's Eyes*, Almscliffe: reach out from a pocket at the back of the feature . . .

2. use two pockets in the roof as undercuts, feet pressing into the back wall . . .

3. at full span you find a pinchgrip on the lip, then press one foot into the pocket you're using as a handhold . . .

4. and reach round the overhang to the jug.

around on a tied-off knifeblade tapped behind some deteriorating limestone flake. Many of the big roofs are still unfreed. Perhaps the most special of these is *Kilnsey Main*, a daunting aid test-piece in its day, scheduled perhaps for a new lease of life as one of the really hard free roofs of the 'French-style' era.

It's surprising what a bit of persistence can do. *The Hollywood Bowl*, a twenty metre roof at Giggleswick Scar in Yorkshire, went free at E6 in 1985. *The Bowl* demonstrates how broad a spectrum of techniques an overhang can demand. Several aspirants, able to do the roof itself, were beaten by a very hard over-hanging wall which leads into the cave, the enormous ceiling of which would probably be impossible but for a kind of bell-shaped internal feature which allows you to get in and bridge your way to the lip. There, two to four metres of upside-down climbing leads to the crux, a desperate 6c pull onto one scabby little hold out to the left, with the top of the route staring you in the face.

Roof technique is everything technique.

In any overhang move get your feet as high as possible on the wall, then keep them on under the roof, using opposed pressure, heel-hooks or foot-jams, whatever you can find. This will extend your reach round the lip. If your feet swing off too soon – especially if the handholds on the lip are small – they may pull your hands off too. Once you have swung free, bring your foot up onto the lip as quickly as you can. Here, you might have to lock off on one arm: either while you reach up with the other hand to get enough height to bring your foot up, or while you squirm into position to heel-hook the lip itself. The sooner you bring your feet up, the sooner you spread your weight and get into balance.

Don't neglect anything that might help, even a bit of friction on the lip. Be flexible in your thinking. The overlap crux of *Silly Arête* (Pant Ifan, Tremadoc), for instance, is best done as a push down and rock over move – eerie, but much more economical than trying to pull up on the crystals above. Overhangs can be lay-backed. A really wide crack in an overhang might call for imaginative work with your knees. Unless you can hang upside-down from the same crack, resting is difficult. On overhangs, try to conserve energy by pacing yourself.

Overhangs encourage rope-drag, but with good management it can be limited. If you place a runner on the back wall of an overhang, extend it properly. I'd rather fall an extra few centimetres than reach the lip and find my ropes have locked solid. In fact, protection is best placed in the overhang itself before you launch out, so that you don't bash into the wall if you come off. Extend that a bit, too, or the rope will be pinned underneath once you get round the lip. Nothing can be done about rope-drag round the lip itself, except to keep the rope out of any crack there. (You can stop the crack off with a runner, but don't use a Friend because the rope may waltz between the cams and end up in the crack anyway.)

If you're using two ropes you can stagger them through the runners to reduce drag – be careful they don't tangle, lift your protection out, or just get irritatingly in the way.

Climbing is the best training for climbing! A classic overhang problem: *Syrett's Overhang* at Almscliffe in Yorkshire. As with any boulder problem, check the landing space for rocks and holes that could break bones. But a committed attempt at an overhang does bring the special hazard of an awkward fall. Your hands may vacate the rock before your foot-jam, resulting in a broken ankle. You are likelier to fall on your head or back. To avoid brain damage or having to wear your neck in a brace, always try to have someone standing in-field. The friendly competitive nature of bouldering tends to encourage this anyway, and in summer evenings at Caley or the Bridestones, the air rings with the cry of 'Watch me back!' Two spotters may be an advantage for a really committing roof move. Overhangs test stomach and arm muscles. In the gym do sit-ups and progress – if you feel lucky – to front levers. For the arms, pull-ups, preferably with some weight. Lock-offs should be done on a fingerboard rather than a bar. The rope ladder is a very efficient training device for overhangs, but for the danger of this and fingerboard work, see Training Section.

Technique: Opposed pressure

Laybacking an arête in the warm evening light, you let your concentration slip a little. In that instant the barn door swings open and you're off. But it's only a couple of metres from the ground. Off among the boulders someone laughs quietly. Suddenly you smell chalk, sweat, dust. If your finger-ends aren't too sore you can get back up and try the move again, once more before it's dark. You weren't going to the top anyway.

Summits are attainable in other ways than climbing to the top, as any tourist will remind you. To that extent rock climbing is no longer to do with getting to the top of anything. It is a celebration of movement for its own sake; of the ability to meter out physical effort in complex, precise ways. In a way it always was. To dismiss modern climbing as 'rock gymnastics' is only to reiterate this.

The move is what we look for now, its subtlety and difficulty: the move is the goal, the new summit. We climb to climb, not to get anywhere.

Is it going too far to say that because of this the history of the sport can often feel like a sack of old books across your shoulders? A kind of moral-weight-training? Tweed-clad Victorians in poses of astonished strain, grimly back-and-footing boxy deteriorating chimneys the size of a horse-drawn bus; red-necks in checked shirts straddling chickenheads under the Colorado sky; Alpine guides dressed with the awful correctness of the Swiss, extending themselves across granite dièdres like open pages from their own interminable autobiographies: their belief in the pointed part of the mountain can seem quaint.

Yet they were inventing in their innocence the opposed pressure techniques subsequently refined into the radical layaways, underclings and bridges of today's 'vertical opera'.

Climbing for its own sake. A millimetre too far on *Great Flake*, E6 6b, Caley Crag.

Soloing *The Rasp* E2 5b, Higgar Tor. Note the right leg extended for balance.

LAYBACKING

Laybacking draws your body against itself like a long-bow. It opposes feet to hands and is designed, like much opposed pressure technique, to take advantage of vertical features and holds. The classic layback is of a flake, or of a thin crack in the back of a corner. Generally, one limb is moved at a time. Laybacking is a strenuous technique, driven by the big muscles in the thighs, shoulders and upper arms; but remember that it can require a sense of balance as well.

Keep your feet high for the transmission of power, low to conserve energy (you pay your money and you take your choice). Be prepared, anyway, to move them about (a) to make use of any footholds that appear, even swinging into a bridged position with one foot on either wall of a corner; and (b) to counteract the barn door. Barn-dooring is one of the two disadvantages of laybacking. The feature you are laybacking acts as a hinge: a sudden, exponentially-increasing swing in the wrong direction cancels out the mechanical energy which was pressing your hands and feet on the rock. The other danger is that you will simply run out of strength and let go. Laybacks – especially fingertip laybacks – are best done fast, 'pure' laybacking avoided when possible. You can operate a layback without flake or corner, using any combination of hand- and footholds that looks likely. Oppose your fingers in an old peg crack to your feet on sloping ledges to either side of it, for instance.

Laybacking arêtes

Laybacking arêtes is a less brutal but more intense experience demanding psychic rather than physical energy. One of the 'last great arête problems' of a few years ago was called *Ulysses' Bow*. In the guise of even more radical arêtes, Penelope still attracts her suitors, but these days they try to pull the bow less by strength than by a mixture of cunning, high-fibre diet and keeping their weight over their feet.

The blunter and more vertical an arête gets, the harder. In this situation you find yourself using the arête itself as a handhold rather than a foothold feature (though sometimes you will need it for heel-hooking as an aid to balance), leaning away from it just enough to direct your weight onto your feet. In a way you're stepping up in balance, using your hands to steady yourself. Reject nothing in the way of footholds. You can often put your weight on a foothold a metre or so in from the arête itself, as long as you keep your hands low. If you try to do this at full stretch you will barn door off.

An arête is the most efficient hinge for the barn door, so beware. Some arêtes will require you to switch sides constantly and fluently. Hold a dialogue with your

1. Look for rugosities that might help footwork.

2. A part-pinchgrip supplements palming and keeps the barn-door shut.

3. Do the same again until you get to the top.

arête, not a monologue: if you set out determined to stay on one side of it the conversation may end suddenly.

Some arêtes have to be climbed facing straight-on, pinch-gripping with the hands and squeezing with the thighs. Even on these it's possible to get some help by laying away a little to one side or the other. No one can literally pinchgrip a ninety-degree arête; the biggest hands just pop off. But the moment you shift your weight a little to one side you get some help. Layaway to the left to help the right hand pinchgrip, then over to the right for the other. You can be pressing with one leg harder than the other, too, in a kind of hook move.

Bridging, Burbage South, Derbyshire.

BRIDGING

Bridging is one of the least instinctive techniques, with no relationship to the 'reach and pull' solutions of the non-climber. The classic bridge is across a smooth vertical corner with no holds in it. The legs of the climber, acting like the cams of a Friend, redirect the vertical energy of bodyweight to push the feet against the walls. It isn't the first thing you'd think of if you wanted to climb something. . . .

Look for rugosities, tiny changes of angle, vertical cracks, anything to get your feet against. Where there is nothing, try to get as much of your sole on the rock as possible: as with slabs, friction will be important, and a smearing boot might be an advantage. Bridging with straight legs is strenuous – touch a knee to the rock for a bit of a rest or to aid balance. Palms press the walls too: I try to keep my hands horizontal, rather than have the fingers pointing up or down – the heel of your hand has tougher skin! – but obviously if there are features you adjust to use them. A crack in the back of the corner can be useful for you hands, but don't be drawn into a layback for more than a move or two. It's uneconomical. (Techniques blur into one another however hard you try to keep them apart, and the number of half-bridge, half-layback moves you do – little swinging shifts of weight, little dabs of the toe on the rock – when you think you are making 'pure' use of one technique or the other must be quite high. In the end climbing is only movement.)

Remember that you can use both hands on one wall, or both feet; or in trying circumstances, both feet on one wall, both hands on the other.

First ascent of *Yosemite Wall* E5 6a, Malham. Strenuous underclinging.

An undercling problem on Stanage. The crunch comes when you have to let go of this undercling!

UNDERCLINGS AND LAYAWAYS

Undercutting and underclinging make use of a downward-pointing flake, small overlap, or similar feature. Lean out from the flake, walk your feet up, and to lock yourself into place, *pull*. The steeper the ground, the less weight will be on your feet, so you must pull harder, especially if you are on smearing holds. The most efficient way of bringing the useful muscle groups – biceps and triceps – into play is to keep your upper arm at ninety degrees to the forearm. This is also the least tiring way of doing it.

Undercuts are only upside-down holds. Incuts are therefore easy to use, square-cut or rounded edges less so, demanding correspondingly more finger strength. Get up over them so that you can really pull on them; and pull upwards rather than outwards.

Undercut holds have a history of radicalization. Classically, they were recommended not as positive holds but as aids to balance. But that was the gentlemanly way, and their evolution since has been savage. Nowadays use them to bunch up tight with your feet a few centimetres from your hands, and thus extend your reach. You can undercling quite a rounded horizontal break by palming it.

The layaway, a subtler cousin of the layback, allows you to use a vertical or 'sidepull' hold for a similar purpose. It consists basically in the shifting of your weight to one side of your vertical axis by leaning away from a handhold and a foothold on the opposite side. Again, in its gentlemanly form it tended to be used for balance.

It's amazing how high a foothold you can use with a layaway; and at this point, with your arm at waist-height or below, you can often turn it into an undercling, even though you're using a vertical hold. With your wrist twisted at the right angle and very heavy pressure from the relevant muscle-group, you can make much better use of a layaway to lock-and-reach than you could a normal fingerhold – particularly on very steep or overhanging ground. The trick is to pull inwards, towards your body, so that foot and hand are opposed as they are in an undercling – the layaway thus becomes a very economic one-hold unit, push, pull and reach.

(You can also use underclings and layaway holds at quite extreme reaches, to aid a step up.)

Green Death Direct Start: the climber's weight distributed between right foot and right hand: a hard balance problem.

GROOVES

Grooves force you into situations simultaneously precarious, awkward and absurd, a combination with high nightmare value matched only by off-width cracks.

Lacking internal features, too flared to get in, too shallow to be bridged, too eccentric anyway in the angles of their sides, they exist somewhere in the gap between a very shallow corner and a very vague chimney. About all you can say is that they are a concave rather than a convex feature, and they encourage an *ad hoc* response, usually contrived from opposed pressure technique.

The main problem is that power must be transmitted eccentrically. Almost by definition, none of the surfaces of the groove are at a good angle for opposition. *The Quarrymen*, Johnny Dawes' test piece on Welsh slate, is a classic modern groove, flared, totally smooth, and constantly twisting around. This reduces you to partial bridges, chaotic back-and-footing, very strenuous hand-and-footing: or a combination of all three. All the time you are fighting the flare, often in more than one dimension. Get whatever you can – shoulder, arm, knee, heel – on the rock and push on it, and hope it will stay there. This isn't just tiring and painful, it can be desperately awkward – so flexibility is your best ally.

Grooves force you to be inventive. Otherwise there's nothing much to add but 'Good luck'.

A Streetcar Named Desire: locking his arms, the climber *jumps* both feet up. A classic problem at Joshua Tree, California.

RESTING/TRAINING TIPS

Opposed pressure makes resting difficult. Laybacking an arête, you can lock yourself in place with a heel-hook and shake out one hand at a time. To rest from a bridge, look for holds; or oppose one foot to both hands – or a shoulder – to allow you to shake the other out. Classic laybacks are very difficult to get a rest from: though with care one limb can be shaken out, this usually puts further strain on the others. Underclings don't really allow a rest – hope there's only one move and that you can do it first time.

On the other hand, opposed pressure can be a method for resting from other techniques. On an overhanging wall, for instance, which requires power-climbing from the upper body, you can rest by bridging on a couple of vertical ribs. You can sometimes swing into a bridge from a strenuous layback. The traditional back-and-foot is associated with resting.

But opposed pressure climbing is generally demanding, so your best rest is to be fit. Bridges take it out of your calf muscles, layaways and underclings tire the responsible arm-groups, grooves punish your back and stomach as well as legs. Do sit-ups and the calf raise and weighted pull-ups for power; circuits for stamina. Bridging and groove-climbing demand flexibility, especially in the hips; ballet- and yoga-based stretching exercises will be valuable here, but don't overdo them or you risk muscle and ligament damage. It's no good being bashful about them one week then committing yourself to the works the next. Climbers who have put on a lot of quick muscle are very vulnerable here.

Resting on a knee bar across a groove.

Technique: Jamming

Classic hand-jamming on *The File*, Higgar Tor . . .

You can get anything from your little finger to half your body in a crack, not that in either case you're going to feel massively secure. Often painful (though it oughtn't to be), difficult to learn and at first to trust, jamming is technique at its least innocent, the antithesis of climbing a ladder or a tree. Until its invention, hand technique was only a sophistication of what a child or a top-sailor already knew how to do – a couple of quick grabs. With jamming and its immediate application to the most extreme possibilities suggested by it, something quite new was added to the toolkit, and climbers would have less in common with scaffolders from then on.

The modern development of the hand-jam has been variously credited. Traditional candidates are Peter Harding (a Peak District climber said to have refined it specifically for use at Cratcliffe Tor and Cromford Black Rocks) and Joe Brown. Both deployed it late in the forties, and which of them came first now seems immaterial. Controversies like these are made not by the principals but by their supporters. As Brown himself said in another context, 'That we made no claims ourselves did not alter the situation; other people had done it for us.' The jam worked well on gritstone, where its use quickly became endemic and climbers celebrated the freedom it brought with a crack-based wave of exploitation which left the crags looking like Sainsburys at the end of a busy Saturday.

By the sixties everyone had found something on the shelves, and the university hopefuls were showing their grit rash to girls in bus shelters: to be hard you had to jam. Much of the myth of Brown and Whillans, then at its public height, was the myth of shredded skin – *The Rasp, The File, The Mincer*, the names tell it all. Twenty years later: nothing. No new hard jamming routes are being put up in Britain because we've run out of new cracks. Cracks like *The Crack* at Froggatt aren't really jam-cracks at all but power/layback problems. Cracks turned out to be a non-renewable resource, and the special skills they brought forth are history. The hard cracks are the old cracks.

. . . and equally classic finger-cracking on *Coventry Street* E4 6b, Millstone Edge.

FINGER CRACKS

In Britain finger-jamming was a late product of the crack-climbing era, re-opening the new-route super-market for a time, and signalling that we would soon be moving back onto the walls. The finger crack breaks down the traditional separation between face- and crack-climbing. Footwork along a line of shallow, bashed peg sockets – spread along some seam originally mined on tied-off razor-blades by Biven and Peck – will most likely be face footwork: toes smeared into depressions, edging holds on either side. The vaguer a peg crack becomes the more halfway-house it is to climb.

Basic finger-cracking is like placing Rock 8s: you look for a suitable neck in the crack and use it to stop your wedged knuckles. (However hard you argue that your fingers slid accidentally down the crack onto it, *using* a Rock 8 or Friend for this purpose is considered unsporting.) But what makes finger-cracking complex is that cracks come at odd angles, thus forcing you to accept unhappy or uncomfortable finger placements and odd, strained wrist positions; flared, so that you can hardly be said to be jamming at all; or parallel-sided, so that you get no aid at all from necking-down.

The less neck there is to a crack the more you will have to cam your knuckles to make them hold. Energy is needed to stabilize a finger-jam. Ideally, get your three largest fingers in the crack, thumb *down*, to the depth of the first or second knuckle, then torque them into place by twisting your wrist. Keep your elbow down as you pull up on the jam, to maintain the torque. The smallest size you can handle like this is obviously dependent on the size of your fingers, but it isn't going to be much less than 1½ cm. Narrower cracks which reject even the first knuckle may accept the hand thumb *up* instead. In this case the little finger is acting like a nut and you can pull straight down on it. Try and stack your ring and middle fingers on top of the little finger to spread the load and get more of your forearm muscle into play. You can reach higher with your thumb upwards.

A wider jam is available: place the thumb below the fingers and torque with the wrist – this, traditionally known as 'spragging', seems insecure until you have done it a few times, but can come in very useful.

Having your thumb up or down changes the position of your forearm and wrist in relation to the rock. Sometimes 'up' or 'down' won't be determined so much by the quality of the jam you can get as by architectural limitations. For instance, if a corner crack has a bounding wall on the left, you will be confined on that side, and forced to use your left hand thumb-up and your right hand thumb-down, whether you want to or not. A layaway, or even a layback, would decrease the effort of getting a thumb-up jam into this sort of crack.

1. A jammed index finger. The remaining fingers stacked on top, thumb torquing on edge of crack.

4. A line of solution pockets that thinks it's a crack. Be flexible.

2. Cram as many fingers in as you can and twist them.

3. Two good fingers are better than three poor ones.

'Up' or 'down' will also determine the position of your wrist and arm in relation to your body, and this too might become a factor in the selection. A fingerjam must hold steady as you go up past it, so it is no good choosing one which will be uncammed by the very movement of your arm as you climb; or which requires uneconomic effort of the wrist to keep it *in situ*. Think your fingerjams out because they just won't work by scrabbling and rushing. Good footwork will give you time to think.

5. Part-jam, part-hold: the wedged index finger stabilizing the others while the thumb pulls **down**.

Above: Toe-torque in a thin crack.

Left: Classic foot-jamming on gritstone.

FOOT JAMMING

If a thin crack is unaccompanied by holds on the face, it should be toe-jammed. Irregularities like flared peg sockets will accept part of the toe of the boot. (A nice pointed toe, perhaps designed for limestone pockets, is useful here.) Poke it in, outside ankle downwards, then twist to press the toe firmly into the pocket. This is a version of the smear, and it will give adhesion in quite shallow indentations.

Smearing is also the key to a crack too narrow for toe-jamming. Here, you must smear the edge of the boot into the crack. Use the inside edge, toe-down, if the crack is in a low-angle wall; the outside edge, heel-down, when the crack steepens. (In the latter case *keep* the heel down when you're moving up). If you're doing this properly you may find it hurts. . . .

The classic foot-crack is the one which accepts the front part of your boot if you turn it over slightly. The boot then cams into position as with the toe-jam, and your bodyweight maintains the torque, making it easy to do and cheap on energy – ideal for resting, although a radical twist can be unpopular with your ankles. Again, keep the heel low when moving up.

The twisting foot-jam is perfect for cracks up to hand-jam width. After that, the broad part of the foot should be fitted in horizontally, pushing it inwards and relying partly on the friction of the rand to wedge it there. Wider still (just off-fist), and you can make a jam by bending your ankle so that its outside is opposed to the inside edge of the boot.

OFF HAND JAMS

Eventually the crack becomes too wide to be finger-jammed but too narrow to admit your hand. Several solutions present themselves, but this remains one of the hardest widths to jam confidently. Try wedging the fleshy part of the fingers – down below the second knuckle – into the crack. Your thumb should be down, your wrist low. Then using your forearm as a torque wrench, twist the fingers against the side of the crack. Torquing like this is strenuous, so the more fingers you can get in the crack, the easier you make it for yourself, by spreading the load.

Alternatively you can thumb-lock. When you contemplate the idea, thumb-locking seems brutal; but though it is more difficult to place successfully, a thumb-lock is actually less strenuous to use. Insert your thumb vertically into the crack, bend it over, and then lock the forefinger on top of it, letting the other fingers come in on top as they will. Pulling down on your fingers will combine with forearm-torque to keep this jam surprisingly firm. It will work better in simple, straightforward placements.

The next possibility is the jammed knuckle. Find an irregularity or neck, and stack two or three knuckles across the crack above it. Curling the fingers into a little fist will automatically expand the knuckles and wedge them against the sides of the crack. This is best done with the palm facing into the rock, and the fingers tucked into the hand. More often than not, a knuckle jam will be painful.

In an awkward position, where the rock-architecture compels you to jam thumb-up, get the hand in as far as it will go and then *lever* against the crack, using the back of your hand as the pivot, so that your fingertips are pressing against the other side. This is a powerful method, a variation on which is to wedge the fleshy part of your hand just below the little finger. None of this will do you any good once your hand goes in past the 'dreaded inch and a quarter': rattling about in the gap between the biggest knuckle and the smallest hand, we are all on our own.

Off-handing gritstone.

A beautiful hand-jam . . .

HAND AND FIST JAMMING

If the crack will accept only your hand, flat, fingers raised, then use it like a nut: wedge it against the taper of the crack. If the crack is slightly wider, tuck the thumb across the palm to fatten your hand up. (Along with the fist-jam this is the 'bombproof' jam, the one you can hang from forever – except that the energy is going into it from your forearm muscles, so unless it's wedged against a taper or a neck in the crack, your hand will eventually get tired. This is worth remembering on overhanging cracks.) If folding your thumb across still leaves the jam sloppy, torquing may help: keep your weight off your hand while you wriggle about, though, or you will have an embarrassing rash to explain in the gymnasium next day.

The widest hand-jam you can make opposes the fingertips and heel of the hand on one side of the crack to the back on your knuckles on the other. Woe betide you if it slips with your weight on it. Some security can be gained by folding the thumb over the index finger.

The fist jam comes in three sizes. Make an ordinary fist and wedge it (again, a neck or taper to the crack will help). This is the basic jam and you can do it in both horizontal and vertical cracks; you can do it palm in or palm out, according to the occasion. For a jam about 2 cm wider, move the thumb out to where it can press against the side of the forefinger. When a very tight fist-jam is required, fold the thumb across the palm so that the tip is between the little and ring fingers, and make the fist round that. Some people find this difficult because of their bone structure. It will make a jam somewhat smaller than the widest hand-jam and more secure.

Look for internal features in the crack: a bulge, a partial neck, an edge or rugosity, a lip you can jam outwards against, will all aid a difficult jam, especially a wide one. Eccentric or partial jams can be made up on the spot. Be imaginative. Your hand isn't quite as adaptable as the cams of a Friend, but it will manage some flare in a crack, and in the end, pain's the only limitation.

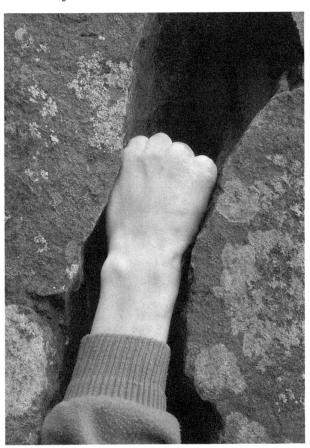

. . . and a bomb-proof fist-jam.

Foot-torquing *Goliath*, E4 6a, Burbage South.

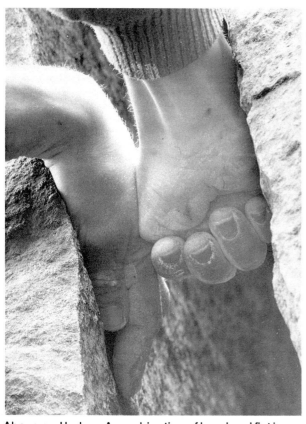

Above and below: A combination of hand and fist jams.

Above: A leg torque – no hands!
Below: Fixing something – whatever works best!

Off-width cracks

Arm-barring in an off-width crack.

There are relatively few off-width climbs in Britain. Because of this, British climbers find off-widthing a bit of a nightmare, whereas in America the technique has been polished into an art.

To make an arm-bar, insert the arm and shoulder as far into the crack as possible. Bend the elbow and push the palm of the hand against one side of the crack; your shoulder presses against the other. This is the classic but strenuous method of using your arm off-width. The forearm lock, less useful, but less tiring, too, is done with the elbow fully bent, palm up, to make the same sort of wedge. A variation of the arm-bar designed for wider cracks has the arm fully bent at the elbow and the hand almost opposite the shoulder. Wider cracks can also be tackled with a version in which the elbow points upwards and the fingers downwards – useful for resting because so little energy is needed to keep it in place.

A leg-bar in an off-width crack.

In a slightly narrower crack, this method might be augmented by knee-locking. Bending the leg at the knee expands the thigh muscles, thus wedging them into the crack.

The outside or trailing leg and foot shouldn't be ignored. Try and find small holds or smears on the walls – especially on overhanging rock, when keeping the outside leg in the crack might unbalance you. Or make a heel-to-toe jam across the outer edges of the crack, remembering to keep your heel low and twist the foot inwards to stiffen it. A wider crack can call for the more specialized version of heel-to-toe known as T-stacking: in T-stacking, both feet are placed inside the crack, one facing in, the other facing across to make the shape of a T. Its advantage is obvious.

A deep reach. If the crack narrows towards the back it may be possible to reach right in for a hand or fist jam, or a vertical edge that can be used as a layaway.

Be careful which way you face in an off-width crack. If one edge of it is off-set, put your back against it; if the crack leans, face into the lean not away from it. In a vertical crack face the most useful-looking edge: generally, the trailing or outside arm pushes or palms where it can. Keep it low or it will become tired.

The most important factor in successful off-widthing is rhythm. All the methods described here seem – and will feel – awkward if you have not used them much. But practice makes them more familiar, and you can soon generate a rhythm of arm-bar/T-stack, leg-bar/palm off. It will never be like climbing a ladder but it may come to seem less uncomfortable.

RESTING

Jamming can be strenuous. Look ahead for possible rests, as you would when laybacking. Try and get your weight onto your feet. A feature inside a crack might allow you to stand for a minute; so might a face hold or a nip in the crack. Where they cut across a vertical crack,

A 'crack machine'.

the eroded bedding-planes of gritstone, sandstone and granite are ideal for this. You can use a knee-lock to rest on, wedging the muscle of the thigh, but be careful because it can be hard to release again, and you don't want to have to be winched off the route! A wide foot-jam is a rest; twisting foot-jams, especially highly-cammed ones, aren't recommended.

On steep ground and overhangs it's hard to rest your arms. Give the muscles a break by jamming with a straight arm, thus transferring the weight to the bones and joints – never try to rest with a bent arm, because the muscles will still be working. Deadhanging like this with one arm allows you to 'shake out' the other. Let it hang loose from the shoulder, keep it low to maximize blood-circulation, shake it about and wiggle the fingers – all this will pump oxygen into the muscle tissue to reinvigorate it. Alternate the arms until both are re-covered. ('Recovery' is a relative concept here. You are never going to be as fresh as when you started out, and sometimes it's better to get going again as soon as possible. Your best rest is at the top.) You can get a good rest hanging from a fist-jam this way, particularly if the crack is necked.

A change is as good as a rest. If you switch briefly from a jam to some other kind of hold – look for possibilities inside the crack or on the wall outside it – you will bring slightly different muscles into play, giving yourself if not precisely a rest then the feeling of one.

TRAINING TIPS

The best training for jamming is jamming. Some indoor walls have cracks. American climbers use 'crack machines' (see left). These contraptions, a carpenter's nightmare, have an advantage over the fixed cracks of a climbing wall: they consist of a set of wooden forms, adjustable from finger- up to off-width cracks. They look odd, but they will deliver any kind of crack at any angle. Levvittation was invented at the famous 'Parking Lot Cracks' in California. In Britain we make do with bouldering for variety; and for the strength and stamina necessary to jam, repetitive top-roping.

Not precisely a problem of training, although it certainly applies to climbers who do a lot of climbing, is that of simple wear and tear due to jamming. Jam properly, they say, and you shouldn't hurt yourself. But that dictum applied to 'classic' cracks, and not all jams follow it. The 6a start to *Jankers Groove* on Froggatt, for instance, depends on a vicious rotating fist-jam. You pull up on it, then outwards, then finally push down on it – every seperate movement taking another layer of skin off! Gaining support every day among Britain's committed climbers is the aerosol skin used in hospitals.

Equipment

HISTORY AND EVOLUTION

In the beginning they went out four or five at a time in tweed suits and nailed boots; tied together but not to the rock, with hemp. 'Belaying', in this programme for disaster, was a matter of taking a turn or two round a spike. This would hold a falling second, but not necessarily two, and rarely a leader. One down, all down. The leader never falls.

I don't see this as admirable in itself. It's only when falling becomes thinkable if not precisely advisable that the basic level of difficulty is first raised, then pushed out like a springboard from which more isolated feats can be performed by the divine madmen of the day, whose craziness we sanction because it gives a glimpse of things to come.

Tying onto the crag to belay, an Edwardian innovation which didn't become widespread until after the Great War, began this process of evolution. The use of gym shoes encouraged better footwork (though tricouni-nails were still superior for edging, and – significantly perhaps – still though of as the 'ethical' technology for the job.) Climbers began to prefer the lighter weights of hemp, which reduced drag and increased managability; and the shoulder-belay, precursor of the back-belay still in use in the sixties. The best protection, though, was still to pass the leader-rope behind a spike and hope it stayed there. If you wanted to use a chockstone or a sling you had to untie, pass the rope through, then tie on again.

These improvements initiated a period of bold climbing. Basic standards rose: VS leads were common: a handful of routes now graded Extreme were established.

After World War II hawser-laid nylon ropes became available. Their higher breaking strain and energy-absorbing stretch, in conjunction with the safer back-belay, further sophisticated rope technique. Hand-placed pebble chockstones and slings pre-tied from different lengths and diameters of nylon line gave birth to the modern runner. Vibram boots replaced nails, but Woolworth's black-soled pumps, worn tight to reduce lateral torsion, remained the smearer's choice. Heavy steel ex-WD karabiners were unreliable under load, but climbers were hungry for experience: out went their necks.

Development accelerated through the fifties and sixties. Kernmantel rope, stronger because of the parallel fibres inside the sheath, began to oust hawser-laid. Drilled machine nuts were threaded on nylon line to replace pebbles; they were soon outdated by com-mercially produced hexagonals and wedges mounted on rope or swaged wire slings. Alloy karabiners were imported from Europe. Crude descenders appeared, though early accidents delayed their acceptance. But perhaps the biggest step forward came when the PA friction boot left its hideaway in Kent, where it had been used to turn sandstone into a kind of parochial Fontainebleau-from-home, and was adopted by Joe Brown. Brown had started in tricounis, like O. G. Jones. He had led *Great Slab* on Froggatt in pumps. Now he was free.

Improvements in the technology of nylon webbing led to very strong tape slings; also to Don Whillans's sit-harness, designed in the early seventies to replace the waist-belt and direct waist tie and reduce the danger of internal damage in a long fall. Along with Chouinard's improvement of the wired wedge – 'stoppers' – and the hexagonal – 'polycentrics' – and the adoption of the dynamic belay-brake, the sit-harness made truly modern climbing possible. The polycentric didn't just wedge against the taper of the crack: it *cammed*. But in the mid-seventies experiments with active camming devices gave rise to the Friend – fast, self-adjusting protection that would operate even in a flared crack. The climbing shops wouldn't accept them at first. Too complex, they said; anyway, 'real' climbers wouldn't take to them.

'Real' climbers wouldn't use gymnasts' chalk either, but grinning ironically through a choking wave of it, the decade went out at around E6 6c. Modern climbing had arrived. Since, we've seen it sophisticated further by the arrival of sticky rubber soles, developments of the wired wedge like Rocks, and recently a new wave of active cam development. We climb with the products of a hundred-year dialectic between safety and ambition: with each improvement in protection or rope-work, *un*protected standards have risen. For tens of thousands of climbers, leading is no longer a repression, but an expression, of the self.

Russell Stephenson and F. Morshead in 1863 wearing the climbing equipment of the day.

Martin Atkinson 1986.

A mixed bag of HBs and Rock Anchors.

PROTECTION

How to be prepared without being encumbered? At 285 grams, a Hexentric 11 weighs 50 grams more than a Friend 4. If protection that large is necessary, which to rack is no real decision: weight is too important. Harder to assess is what you will need – especially in the middle range, say 20–30 mm – for a given on-sight lead. Generalizations are a trap. So are fashions. Use your eyes: don't take knee-knockers on a slab: equally, don't rack two RPs and a half-size Friend for a 30 m by 30 mm crack. Listen for the gossip, the local knowledge that tells all about hidden or minimal placements.

A few roped runners might turn out useful. They are less amenable than a Friend, and not much good in flared cracks. On the other hand – unless you have the compact 'Technical' Friend – a roped nut will take better advantage of a shallow placement; and a 'keyhole' placement will utilize a limestone pocket that won't accept a Friend at all – flip the Hex in along its long axis, then turn it ninety degrees to lock it. The

A well-bedded Moac Original, grandfather of modern nuts.

1. Rock 7 on wire in a conveniently necking crack.

2. Rock 2 on wire, with the wire in a good position.

A selection of wired rocks.

larger Rocks can be handy. Pre-taped Rocks are wider than ordinary ones; and even though tape is stronger than perlon they don't seem popular in Britain.

(The same is true of Kevlar, a high-tech 'accessory cord', thinner, lighter and perhaps stronger than perlon. While doubts about its durability and its strength round a small radius have recently been answered encouragingly by tests at Chouinard Equipment, its use on roped runners isn't widespread.)

Below 15–20 mm, all your protection will be wired. Probably the most efficient wire is the Rock. A simple-profile wedge, like the old Stopper, works well only when its taper matches that of the crack. Rocks are designed with complex concave-convex curves to overcome this. They seat more securely. They enable advantage to be taken of an irregular crack. On a British wall route, Rocks 1–5 will be the most useful sizes. I double- or even treble-up on the first three.

Refine your racking system and learn it. On-sight leaders often rack a dozen or more wires on two or three carrying-krabs. This complicates placement. The correct size must be selected, the nut must be placed and then slipped off the carrying-krab, and the krab returned to the rack – all before the extender can be attached and the rope clipped! To avoid this, carry your wires on individual karabiners on one side of your harness; and on the other a selection of quickdraws, plus a few single krabs to use in low-drag situations.

Rack your wires by size so that you don't fumble. If you have to return one to the rack, keep it in sequence. A harness racking system gives you a better centre-of-gravity than a single bandolier, especially on overhanging rock.

Practise with your wired nuts until you have an instinct for size and placement. The best position for a Rock is a tapered vertical slot that matches the curve of the wedge; the wire should be as vertical as possible too. In a thin horizontal break or pocket that tapers at one end, you can get a surprisingly juicy wire; similarly if its lips close. Good placements won't turn up most of the time, though, so what will you accept?

Be flexible: fish around in the internal irregularities in the crack, but be careful of marginal-edge placements on rugosities or tiny pebbles. They haven't the holding power or the stability. If you suspect instability (with a narrow crack, a suspicion is all you might get!) make sure the runner is well-extended to minimize the effects of rope-drag; or weight it into place with a couple of extra karabiners. In general, place a smaller nut in the back of the crack for stability, rather than a larger one

A well-cammed small Hexentric.

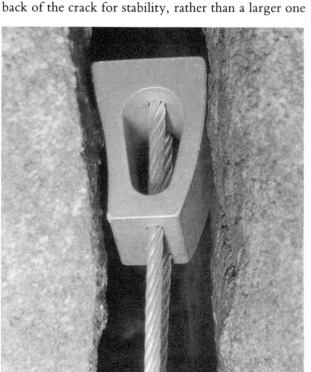

Taking advantage of a curved crack with a wired Rock.

Small Rock on rope.

Placing a microwire on *Coventry Street*, Millstone.

Rock Anchor in use on gritstone.

towards the outside. On limestone, beware of the crack that starts flared, narrows into what looks like a perfect slot, then flares again so that your nut drops through and comes out lower down! Soil packed into the back of a crack can hide this trap. Poke it out with a nut-key or the wire on the Rock you are placing.

Flakes make perfect wire placements: but make sure they're well cemented on!

Early microwires tended to have horrifically low breaking strains, because the wire was thinner, and because it had to conform to a very small radius to go through the nut. RPs, invented for use on Arapiles in Australia, overcame this limitation by silver-soldering the wire directly into a brass head. They came in six tiny sizes, the smallest 3 mm, and their almost square section makes them ideal for shallow placements.

A slightly larger version is the HB, a nut which is tapered in two dimensions and works well in flared cracks. Make sure you put them in the right way round!

One of the disadvantages of microwires is that during the manufacturing process the wire gets heat-treated near the nut. When your second comes to remove them from a deep placement, it tends to be by a ripping motion: this bends and stresses the wire at the critical point, inducing metal fatigue. Check your microwires for little breakages there.

Chouinard tried a steel head for microwires, but now seem to have reverted to brass. I can't recommend the Italian '2-stop'; the wire is far too long and levers the nut out in use. Not available yet but showing considerable promise is Hugh Banner's Rock Anchor, similar to an RP but with a shorter head allowing thicker wire to be used.

Microwires are good in clusters. While it's common to talk as if these clusters can be 'designed' to rip or break in sequence or pattern, thus absorbing fall-

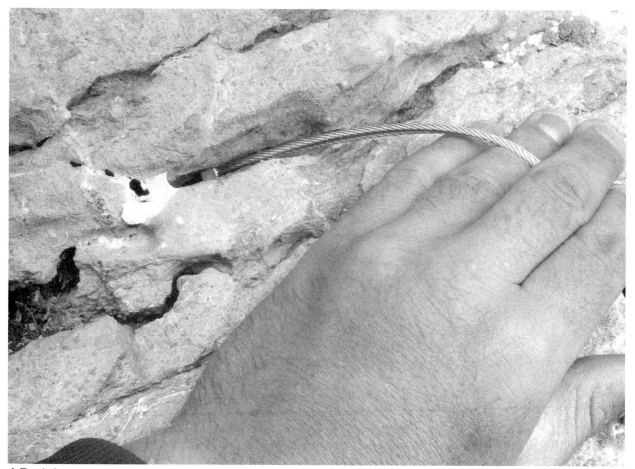

A Rock Anchor in a limestone pocket.

energy, you would have to be rather a good engineer to do this, and the best thing to do is just stick as many of them in as possible. Lace a thin crack with RPs, put a bunch of HBs in nearby. Run a rope through each bunch as if it's one good runner. Tapes designed to rip or unstitch so that they absorb shock have never caught on in Britain.

An HB in a solid limestone placement.

3 Friends

An overtight placement for a Friend 1.

Cammed protection: active and passive

The best parallel-crack protection works by transmitting fall-energy to the sides of the crack, so that the harder you fall the better it bites. Passive Cam Units – the Chouinard Polycentric, the Lowe TriCam which looks like a small pig on a tape – do this by twisting. Active Cam Units such as the Friend, the Go-Pro Roller, and the Metolius 3-Cam, transmit the shock mechanically. Quick, self-adjusting protection which would work even in flared cracks! – ACUs were always the climber's wildest dream. So much so that when Friends appeared in Britain in the late seventies, no one could quite believe in them (a comment not so much on engineering as on dreaming).

It should be said immediately that ACUs have their drawbacks, one of which is price. Friends will 'walk' into a crack, powered by the rocking effect of rope-drag. They will not walk out again, which is discouraging at around £30 a throw. If you can't get your fingers to the trigger-bar, don't smash the rock up in your misery. They can be teased out with patience using two wires to operate the triggers. (Climbers with a talent for

this scour Stanage Edge when everyone has gone home, grinning guiltily at one another like vultures.) The real solution to this is not to place them in too deep in the first place; and to extend them well. Try to align the shaft with the direction of fall, canted slightly outwards so that the triggers are accessible.

Cams can become reversed, which does not make them effective. Friends are less compact than an ordinary nut, at the smaller sizes; but developments have made the 'Technical Friend', with its titanium stem, much more compact than the original. In horizontal placements, Friends are best tied off to reduce leverage. Use 4 mm perlon, tied through the first hole above the trigger bar; tape it to the shaft to keep it out of the way.

The newer, three-cam units, from Wired Bliss and Metolius, were designed to fit thinner cracks than the smallest Friend. If Friends, which have four cams, walk into cracks, 3-Cams tend to walk out of them, leaving you more vulnerable than you thought you were. Their cams may rotate out of contact with the rock in a less-than-tight placement. They are also prone to false triggering: if you pull one side of a Friend trigger bar,

Friend 4: get someone else to carry it up for you!

Metolius 3-Cam.

only one set of cams will shift: do the same on a 3-Cam and they all open. (Plans are afoot in Britain for a TCU triggered by a central ring-pull, which will solve this problem.) Because of their frame-like construction, Wired Bliss and Metolius units are better fitted for the kind of deep crack you associate with Yosemite granite; but Rollers, which use a curious wedge-and-cylinder mechanism, are quite compact.

All these devices are more expensive than a Passive Cam Unit. Polycentrics are still ideal for the average climber, just as easy to place at VS or HVS. But they are limited to two or three kinds of placement, vulnerable to irregularities in a crack; and they won't work in a flared crack at all. TriCams, if they were less like juggling, might be a good stage up from Polycentrics. Many British climbers do use the smaller sizes to take advantage of eccentric pocket and shot-hole placements – I did this myself on *Masters Edge* E7 6c at Millstone Edge. But I've found that their more bizarre possibilities need two free hands to exploit; and it seems to me that the combination of a hard metal roller with a softer wedge could lead to the cutting of the one by the other. If the roller slides off the nut at one side, too, you are in trouble.

The first British TCU – the HB.

Extenders and karabiners

In the seventies people still tied their own tape slings, using the old 'tape knot', which came undone a lot. (If you have to replace the tape on original Friends, this will still be necessary. Do stitch the loose ends of the knot down.) This has been outdated by slings and extenders pre-sewn by the extraordinarily strong 'bar tacking' process.

Tape-width can affect the strength of a karabiner: the wider it is, the more leverage it will exert, especially on the 9 mm 'Microlite' type of krab. Petzl have got round this by using for the quickdraws and extenders a cleverly-sculptured tape – fat in the middle for strength, cut away at the ends to be more conformable to the karabiner angles. The other solution is to use the new 14 mm tape which has a breaking strain of 1,800 kilos. (Strong enough. A load of this weight would literally rip you apart anyway.) Tapes go up to around 26 mm wide, with a loop strength of 2,500 kilos. Tie-offs, quickdraws and extenders come either as ordinary loops, or 'express' slings, sewn together in the middle with a loop at each end. I carry mainly short (10 cm) ones, with the odd longer one for extension where there might be rope-drag.

Karabiners work properly only when the gate is closed. Finish can be important here: the tape can catch on an internal lip and in a fall-situation open the gate. We are trying now to smooth off internal contours as much as possible, and to make the critical angles acute so that wherever the tape is lying inside the karabiner it will locate itself properly immediately it comes under load, directing the fall-energy along the back of the krab.

The breaking strain of an open krab – whatever its rating – is about 6 or 700 kilos. You can generate that with a very short drop onto a runner.

Karabiners are becoming increasingly sophisticated. Not so much in terms of strength – those problems were sorted out long ago – but in terms of design-logic, which has been archaic, a hangover from the needs of the old aid-climbers, who had to be able to open a krab under bodyweight. Gates were lightly sprung and tolerances sloppy in the nose area. Now we look for a very high tolerance closing slot which will lock solid under the slightest load. This helps prevent the krab opening if it knocks against the rock – even if the gate is open only for an instant, a fall will *hold* it open, with obvious results. Double-krabbing can open gates, too. A badly-placed peg may force you to put the first krab in so that it sticks out at an angle; the rope lifts the second krab against it, and by a kind of Chinese puzzle trick, flicks it open.

For some Petzl or Troll bolt hangers you need a small karabiner with a narrow nose. Even a modern bolt-ring hanger accepts the krab more easily (and more quickly!) if the karabiner nose is smoothly-shaped and narrow. A

Express extender and two krabs.

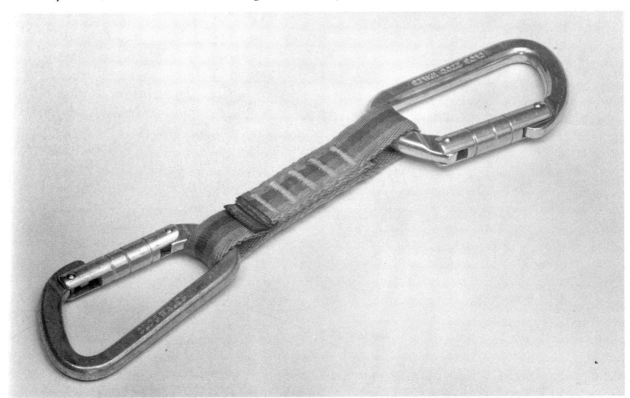

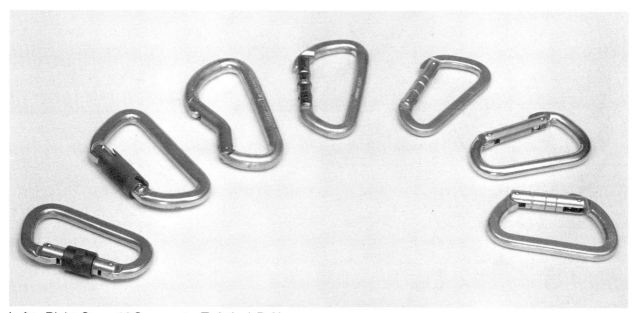

Left to Right: Super 10 Screwgate; Twistlock D; New Alp Bent Gate; Simond Cliff; Hyperlight; Basic 10; Modified 10.

square-cut nose requires two movements instead of one to get it through. At the other end of the quickdraw or extender, a larger krab with a 'banana' gate encourages the rope neatly in.

For belay-brake systems, and for abseiling, 'offset' karabiners are less efficient; an oval, more symmetrical shape prevents the rope from binding up in the tight corners, especially if you are double-roping.

Clipping a bolt: note the slim, narrow-nosed karabiner at the business end.

Single-roping on *Rasp Direct* E3 5c, Higgar Tor.

ROPES

A good modern rope will have – in addition to high breaking strain and energy absorption – ease of handling, abrasion-resistance, light weight, and some resistance to ultra-violet degradation. It may also be treated with 'super dry' coatings to prevent absorption of water. You pay more for these, and the first time you abseil on one they melt off; they make the rope harder to manage and to knot.

A modern rope costs a lot and is as vulnerable to sharp objects, household and industrial chemicals, as an old-fashioned one. Discourage people from standing on yours, and your dogs or children from chewing it. There is an increasing use of rope-bags to protect the investment from both physical and UV damage. Don't store rope on the back shelf of the car where the sun can get at it. After sea cliff climbing, wash it (this will not strip out 'valuable oils': it is not a guernsey sweater) at the same time as your karabiners and Friends.

By using a single rope to climb on you are gaining simplicity of handling, weight reduction and strength. 11.5 mm rope is obviously the strongest, 11 mm still the most common. But 10.5 mm is already in use for hard climbing, to save weight, and there will soon be easily available 10 mm ropes as strong as 11 mm or 11.5 mm, but with very tough, abrasion-resistant sheaths. (A single rope, obviously, leaves you prone to the effects of damage.) Single-roping is aesthetically pleasing, and exciting, too. You are naked while you're clipping the runner – no back-up from the second rope – and the fall distance has increased by the amount of slack you have out.

Its drawbacks are obvious, though. Don't let its sudden fashionability tempt you into using it where double-roping would be more efficient. It hardly seems possible in 1987 that climbers should have to be reminded that zig-zagging with a single rope will increase drag and dislodge runners; and that a fall onto a zig-zagged rope is likely to strip every runner but the last: and yet I saw quite recently a picture of someone doing a full body-bridge above a system like this on the *Devil's Tower* in Wyoming. High-tech climbing, low-tech brains. Use extenders freely in this situation. Drag also increases with the number of bolts in a route: a seven or eight bolt route is ideal for single-roping, anything more is less so.

Top-roping is usually done on a single rope. Use 10.5 or 11 mm. It's not only stronger, it stretches less; constant stretching will damage a 9 mm rope.

The other drawback is retreat. With a 50 m rope you can abseil only 25 m. A lot of modern European routes (and increasingly some British ones) have a fixed lower-off point at the top: if the route's over 75 m you're in trouble. People are killed every year by fast lowers in situations like this. Make sure that your second either ties a knot in the end of the rope to stop it shooting through or (safer) actually ties onto the rope as in traditional climbing.

Double-roping has major advantages. It relieves drag on traverses, and eliminates zig-zagging. It makes overhangs and sudden changes of direction less fraught. It enables you to 'favour' a dubious runner – that is, to lessen the shock-load on it by clipping the second runner into an equally dubious piece. It favours dubiously-seated protection, too: clip one rope into the wobbly runner, then use the other for a while so that the drag goes elsewhere. Double-roping makes clipping safer – or at least gives a less naked feeling – and enables you to be lowered from an undependable nut while you are protected by a better one on the second rope. You can abseil further on it.

Its disadvantages seem inconsiderable to the European climber. Double ropework is marginally more demanding, especially if you're cold and tired; there is a slight increase in weight.

A popular method of training is self-top-roping, using a Petzl shunt. The rope is fixed at the top of the route, and weighted or tied down at the other end. The shunt is pushed up a few metres at a time as protection. Two things to remember about this: don't use anything but a Petzl shunt – ascenders, prusik knots and so on are all very unreliable or cause massive rope damage in a fall; and don't grab the shunt as you fall, or you will release it!

Double-roping *Pierrepoint*, Gordale, on a mixture of bolts, pegs and Rock 5s.

HARNESSES

All the basic design and safety problems of the sit-harness have long been solved, so that when buying one your concerns should be elsewhere. Obviously you need strength, but features like weight, durability and comfort are almost as important. If you are going to fall a lot, or sit in your harness for long periods of time, it's wise to remember that 60% of the load is taken by the leg-loops. (One of the major perils of bolt placement is harness chafing; and back-of-the-thigh bruising is now endemic in Britain's hard climbing population. Harnesses now come padded – 'soft' – to alleviate this, but a more fundamental solution may be needed to cure the problem completely.) Fastenings should be an area of concern: 'swami' belts, fastened by tying knots, seem pointless to me now that dependable buckles are available – they are slow, cumbersome, and difficult to tighten properly. Always learn and follow the manufacturer's instructions for fastening, and also for tying on: the best harness will become useless if you don't. Look for high abrasion resistance, and a racking system that suits you.

Below: Gill Fawcett climbing *Oliver* E4 6a, Stoney Middleton.

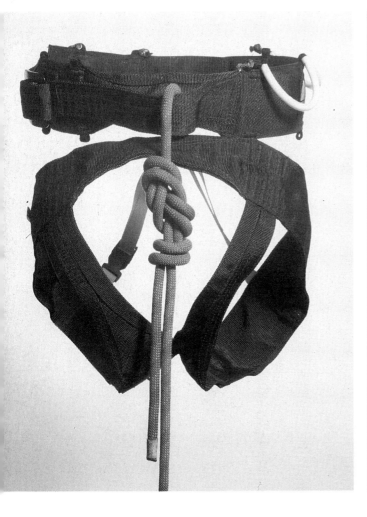

BOOTS

No sooner had Pierre Allain's friction boot been accepted by British climbers than it was elbowed out by the EB, now remembered – more or less fondly – for its narrow last and foetid rubberized-canvas upper. EBs dominated the scene until their manufacturer, pressed by increasing demand and rising costs, went over to mass production. The inferior fit, poor toe shape, and planned obsolescence of the new boot endeared it to no-one, and led directly to an explosion of boot-technology as new manufacturers rushed into the gap.

At first research concentrated on uppers. A comfortable boot, which would at the same time retain the old design compromise between edging and smearing, was much sought after. (It still is, though whether comfort and efficiency can ever be reconciled is debatable. British climbers have always complained about having too broad a foot for the continental last. Yet, since the PA, the top routes of the day have inevitably been done in continentally-designed footwear.) Perhaps the leaders of this period were the Scarpa Cragratz, a fine edging boot; and the Hanwag, a Rolls Royce of comfort, durability and expense.

But by 1981 all bets were off. The Boreal Firé had been born somewhere near Alicante in Spain, out of a cauldron of advanced rubber compounds. Climbing was about to be changed forever by a boot in which construction was subordinated to friction: the upper of the first Firés was makeshift, under-finished, over-stretchy, and like the old EB excruciatingly uncomfortable. The skills had all gone into designing the rubber, a composition so complex that millionths of a gram are critical, and impossible to analyse, even if you know the basic recipe, because of the changes which take place when the compound cools. Too little of the 'tackifying'

Calma Ron Fawcett, flexible and sticky.

Chariots of Firé: no pain, no gain.

Firé Cat, slightly stiffer.

Hanwag Magic Light slipper, with an interesting heel-tension system.

agent and you lose friction; too much and you're left with a hyper-sticky sole so soft it flakes off the boot.

Because of this, though most manufacturers have a version of sticky rubber, none can claim the adhesion of a Boreal or Calma sole. They have concentrated instead on a high-quality, re-solable, all-purpose upper. But comfortable fit isn't necessarily efficient fit – and re-soles are never as good as the original (even if you use Firé rubber) because the re-soler hasn't the last the boot was built on. This kind of footwear is like a sporty family car, a series of compromises in which perform-ance must eventually lose out to durability, comfort, and a boot you can get the pram in. Scarpa Rockstars have a reasonably adhesive sole. Sportivas seem to start out well, but the rubber wears down quickly; a nice fit, as you would expect, but a bit expensive.

Traditionally an edging boot has needed harder con-struction than a smearer – a stiffer sole, an upper built for support (a hangover, in fact, from the thinking behind an Alpine boot). This distinction is breaking down. A really close fit – we are not talking 'comfort'

here – enables the foot itself to stiffen a fairly soft, flexible boot. I wear Firés for everything, encouraging my size 11 feet into a size 9 boot. I'm quite happy to edge in a soft boot, but my ankles and feet are quite strong. I know several climbers who, whatever type or brand of boot they wear, simply keep a new pair for edging, then, as they soften up and the sharp edge goes, turn them over to smearing. Kamet and Hanwag makes boots especially for edging; whereas for a good smear you want a Firé, or the new Calma Lince. Sportivas are quite soft too.

Specialized designs are beginning to make an appear-ance. The Firé Ballet, for instance, has been built for toe-tip edging, with a rounded toe and a lightly elasti-cated heel which pushes your toes down into the front of the boot. This is painful, but it gives a more efficient use of the front edge. A pointed toe is useful for limestone pockets, though by reducing front sole area it radically reduces smearing-power. Sportiva have pro-duced a totally edgeless 'slipper' for radical padding. A more technically advanced version of this idea is the Ninja, a very soft elasticated slipper with a wrap-round Firé sole and a front rand which covers all the toes. They feel like a second skin, and allow you very accurate pocket-to-toe matches! The Hanwag Magic Light is less a slipper than a shoe; like all Hanwags it is beauti-fully built.

It will be interesting to see if, and how, specialized boot-use develops.

A trainer with a sticky sole, designed for quick getaways after bouldering!

Training

INTRODUCTION

Climbing is a complex sport. Strength and endurance are basic to it, but cannot be deployed without balance, flexibility and co-ordination. Technique is rooted in these qualities but can also be seen as a method of managing them. At a further level up, technique is itself only a component, organized by the ability to make decisions under stress. Finally, above the level of psychological skills lie ambition, determination, 'character' – motivational skills which can themselves be trained.

O. G. Jones worked out with weights in the late nineteenth century, but in Britain systematic supplementary training for strength and endurance remained unfashionable until Peter Livesey, who was a county-class runner before he became interested in climbing, began to apply it in the early 1970s. His results were so good that we can't now imagine why the climbers of the fifties and sixties boasted that their only training was forty Woodbines a day and a good spit. More importantly perhaps we can't imagine how they would get up a modern hard route at all.

For a short time, running off a process called glycolysis – the conversion of stored sugars to the magic fuel adenosinetriphosphate – a muscle needs no oxygen. A quick sprint for the bus (you feel you're floating, it's so effortless) is powered by this 'anaerobic' metabolism. If the bus accelerates, and you keep chasing it, lactic acid begins to build up in the muscles as a waste product, causing that burning or 'pumped' sensation. By now you are beginning to pant, because your muscles have been forced to go over to the oxygen-based or 'aerobic' metabolism which burns glucose, glycogen or stored adipose tissue (though they are so reluctant to use the last of these you will have to follow the bus for twenty minutes to switch it on).

Endurance training makes your aerobic systems more efficient. It has the valuable secondary effect for climbers of decreasing the adipose tissue (fat) content of the body, thus increasing power-to-weight ratio.

Strength and *power* are often confused. Strength is the amount of force delivered by a muscle. Power and speed, sometimes called 'explosive strength' are functions related to the nervous system; to the type of muscle fibre (fast or slow twitch) in use; and to the Force × Velocity equation. Strength is what enables you to pull up at all; power is the snap with which you do it, and lies at the heart of the sudden dynamic lurch or 'dyno'.

Balance is the control of the body round its centre of gravity. CG is lower in women than in men, which is why male gymnasts don't bother to compete on the balance bar – they would only totter helplessly about – and why women often climb better on slabs than men. Balance is not limited to slab climbing, but invades every area. *Agility*, the precise and rapid control of balance, diminishes with tiredness as well as with overweight; and with mental as well as physical tiredness. Women are often more agile than men.

Strength programmes can often actually shorten and stiffen muscles, so *flexibility* isn't just important for wide bridging. Flexible muscles have better blood circulation than tight ones; flexible climbers are less prone to injury.

You 'wire' a basic *technique* in the same way you wire a specific move, by practice. A layback is a complex of sensory-motor feedback loops between brain, limbs and muscles, which become more comprehensive and productive as you repeat them. In its role as the organizer of activity, technique works with *co-ordination* to manage the feedback loop between recognition of the problem (a thin nearly-vertical crack in a corner, unjammable) and its solution (the exact layback moves used on the particular climb on the day). Technique and co-ordination are trained on boulders and climbing walls, as are *psychological and motivational skills*. All the endurance in the world won't help you if you can't make a correct decision under stress; or if you overface yourself before you leave the ground. The more difficulties of this nature you meet, the better you will become at handling them.

Unproven methods

Because rock climbing as a sport is comparatively new it has no proven training methods of its own. Two examples of the attempt to design such methods – exercises specific to the climber – have recently caused controversy.

The static deadhang is used in conjunction with a fingerboard or other thin edge for finger-strengthening, and consists – as its name suggests – in simply hanging at full stretch, elbows straight, for longish periods. When you do pull-ups on a fingerboard – or for that matter, fingery moves on a climb – your joints are never actually still. This stimulates the production of synovial fluids for lubrication. In a static hang, no fluids may be produced, and to all intents and purposes bone is grinding on bone.

The Bachar ladder is basically a rope ladder rigged at a slant so that you climb the underside of it. Adjustable rungs mean you can plan for the greatest possible reach, or 'extension'. The problem isn't so much going up a Bachar ladder as coming down it. Lowering hand-only at your full reach is lethal on your elbows: and on a 20 metre ladder you can't just give up and jump off.

Both these training methods have produced excellent results in terms of *training*. But they have also put two of Britain's world-class climbers, Jerry Moffat and Andy Pollit, in hospital with tendon and joint injuries that could be cured only by quite difficult surgery. We are talking here about lay-offs of a year or more. There is a clear case for saying that until we know how – and to what degree – the Bachar ladder and the deadhang encourage injury, we should use them very sparingly indeed, if not avoid them altogether. If you use a fingerboard, do pull-ups; if you build a ladder, build it without massive extension, and low enough to jump off.

In a recent American survey, the majority of climbers were discovered to be suffering constantly from sprains, pulled muscles and inflamed synovial membranes. Some of this is due to insufficient or inefficient training. A lot is due to over-training, even by proven methods, such as endurance traversing on small holds. The strength of tendons and ligaments is hard to improve, and slow; whereas your muscles respond very quickly to any kind of resistance training. This puts you in a situation where you can literally rip your own tendons apart: suddenly, you have all the pull in the world, but they can't handle it. A 'popped' tendon means six months off; the least you'll get is inflammation painful enough to spoil your enjoyment. A broken bone heals stronger than it was originally, but tendons and ligaments never really recover. Don't spend all your time on very small holds – have rest periods in which you try to get all your fingers curled round something; and allow two or three days between very hard training sessions for recovery.

Most prone to injury are climbers who have done *neither* much training nor much climbing. Work up to it slowly. At the beginning, climbing is the best training for training. . .

Martin Atkinson on a Bachar ladder.

Deadhanging.

Warming up

The best way to minimize injury is to warm up before you start. (This applies to climbing as well as training.) If you begin a wall session by traversing twenty metres on 6b holds wearing 4 kilos of divers' weights, you will deserve everything you get: start by doing easier stuff on bigger holds with no weight. One of the major purposes of warming up is to open the small blood vessels in the heart and muscles, preparing them for increased oxygen transport. The most rudimentary way of doing this is to jog – not run – to the gym instead of taking the car. But a warm-up programme should also include some exercises for loosening and stretching the relevant muscles. These exercises shouldn't be 'ballistic', that is quick and vigorous, but should flow smoothly into one another, avoiding sudden changes. Neither should they be done with any kind of weights. Exercise the major joints. During the warm-up, switch the effort from muscle group to muscle group, so that no group ever does more than two consecutive exercises.

Mike Cudahy, ultra-endurance runner extraordinary.

GENERAL ENDURANCE TRAINING

Cardiovascular – aerobic – training is the basis of all fitness. An efficient aerobic system delivers more oxygen, more dependably, to the working muscles. Any aerobic activity should: raise the pulse rate; maintain that increase for between 15 and 20 minutes; and be done often enough (at least three times a week) to persuade the body to adapt to the new demand. The more of your body is involved, the more aerobic stress; the more aerobic stress the higher the gain. Swimming and dance – both of which have flexibility advantages – and cross country-skiing would obviously be more effective here than cycling or running.

Having said this, running has been perhaps the most popular aerobic training for the last ten years. Apart from a decent pair of shoes, it requires no equipment. There are no entry fees – a bonus as far as climbers are concerned – and neither are you hampered by the opening hours of swimming baths or dance centres, etc.

Sporadic bursts of activity don't have a training effect. The key to stamina is not to run forty kilometres once a fortnight, but to do shorter runs at frequent, regular intervals. It doesn't matter how slowly you run in the beginning, or how far, as long as you do the basic 15 to 20 minutes. Unless you intend to take up running as a second sport, you should aim in the end to be doing 5 to 8 km a day at just over 4 minutes per km. Don't get caught up in competitive distinctions between 'jogging' and 'running', especially at the start – you get no worthwhile aerobic effect from going fast, and 'high quality' training is only necessary or useful for competing runners. Long slow distance running (LSD) is the best way to increase general cardiovascular endurance: but if only to alleviate boredom there should be some change of pace. The ideal solution is to run cross-country and on hills, so that your pace is broken up, all the leg muscles utilized, and your feet protected from the fatigue-damage associated with road-running.

A more advanced method of training is the 'interval'. Interval training means breaking up a session with partial rests (good for the anaerobic systems too, since they get the body used to operating in oxygen-debt). Run at, say, 75% of your best speed for five minutes, then slow down to a jog for two, and so on. Hills can do this for you naturally; or alternative high and low mileage runs across a week, hard and soft training weeks. Interval training brings faster results than LSD – but remember that if you run too hard too suddenly, or without proper warming up, you will risk muscle damage. Downhill running on rough country puts considerable stress on your knees – to avoid cartilage problems, do resistance exercises to build up the quadriceps. Make sure, especially if you have to run on roads, you have a properly-built running shoe.

Muscles: strength, power and endurance

Training is about overloading yourself. To develop muscles, you work those you already have against resistance. In *isotonic* training the muscles move against a mobile weight. This may be a dumbell or a barbell ('free weights'); a machine such as a Multigym or Nautilus; or your own bodyweight, as in a pull-up or press-up. Bodyweight is the cheapest resistance you can find. Free weights enable greater selectivity than machines. *Isometric* training pits your muscles against themselves, as with a 'Bullworker' or the classic pectoral exercise in which the palms of the hands press against one another across the heart. Isometrics make for static strength, the kind which helps you hold a locked-off position while you shake out or place a runner. Climbers get plenty of isometric work from actual climbing.

Resistance must be progressive. Body tissues need time to adapt to increased effort: early or excessive overload will cause injury, especially in young or previously unfit people. Strength, endurance and power depend on repetitions, recovery time, and loading. Before you can go on to heavy endurance or power work, you need a certain minimum level of strength. Repetitions are divided into sets, with proper recovery time allowed in between. Start by doing 3 sets of 10 reps each. These decide the correct weight for you to start with: there should be no chance of your managing an eleventh rep! This is called 'momentary muscular failure' and is nature's way of reminding you not to knock any more walls down for a bit.

Exercise the muscle through its whole range. The temptation towards the end of a lengthy session is to skimp on movement, so things become easier: but this loses you much of the benefit. Get someone to check that you are doing the exercise properly. If you shift very heavy weights across a limited range of movements you will end up as beefcake, without agility or snap: the Hollywood Tarzan would have been better at uprooting trees than climbing them. Once you can complete all your sets comfortably, three times in a row, up the weights. To improve, you must keep pushing.

Training is wasted unless it is specific. Climbers tend to need endurance rather than explosive power or absolute strength, though 'dynos' demand the former and feet-off overhangs the latter. A 'needs analysis' looks at the basic movements of the sport and the muscles which power them. At its most schematic, climbing is reach, pull and step up. The forearm muscles clamp the fingers on; the *biceps brachii, teres musculature* and *latissimus dorsi* ('lats') bend the arm and shoulder; knee-extension is accomplished by the *quadriceps*, the big muscle of the thigh. Mantelshelves make

The 'Pec-Deck' – mirror not for narcissistic purposes!

I run on the Peak District moors and along the gritstone edges every day, and often mix training by running between bouldering venues. (There is no reason why low-grade bouldering shouldn't be a form of general aerobic training in itself – stick to big holds, near the ground, turn your Walkman up, and dance!) There's nothing like it in good weather; but it has its charms in rain and gales too: you can *feel* your determination building up as you slog uphill day after day in the mud. This is a side-effect at the level of psychological and motivational skills. There are others: marathon runners are notably skinny, because aerobic stress training burns excess fat – adipose tissue – as fuel. You will find too that it increases not only your endurance but your recovery rate from other forms of physical activity . . .

demands on the lats, and on the *triceps brachii* and *deltoids*. Standing around on slabs and small holds will take it out of the calf group.

Matching exercise with technique means considering the muscle, its range of movement in the climbing situation, and the demands made of it in terms of absolute strength, endurance of explosive power. For instance, if you decide to improve your reach-and-pull climbing, you will want to concentrate on the *biceps brachii, teres complex* and *lats*. Obviously the biceps can be exercised with free weights (Standing Barbell Curls) or machines (Standing Pulley Curls), but a pull-up will not only exercise all the muscles involved, but exercise them in a way that matches their 'real' use on the crag. To pump these muscles, don't hang from your finger-tips – your fingers will tire long before the bigger groups of the arm, back and shoulder. Get your whole hand round the bar. To prevent your stomach muscles unfairly aiding the groups you want to concentrate on, lock your legs as in the picture, with the weight between them. Work for endurance.

A list of useful free-weight and some equivalent

Right: Pull ups with weights.

Inclined sit-ups.

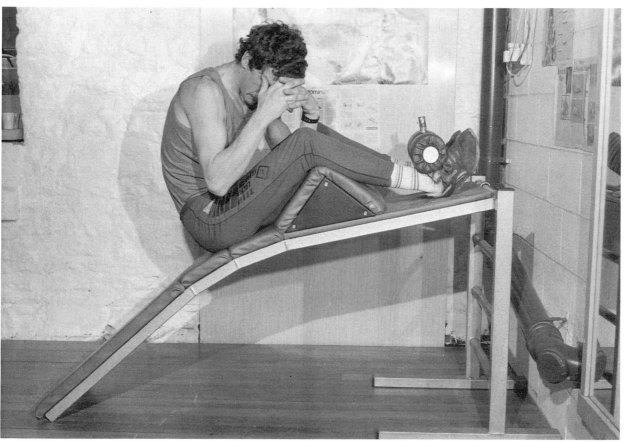

machine exercises might run as follows: for the deltoids, Lateral Dumbell Raises or Machine Presses; for the triceps brachii, Close Grip Bench Presses, or the Triceps Pulley Push Down; for the lats, Front Pull-Ups or Rear Pull-Downs on the machine; for the abdominal wall, Inclined Sit-Ups; for the quadriceps, Front Squat or Barbell Squat with slightly raised heels; for the *gastrocnemius – soleus tibilias* complex, Calf Raises. Forearms can be strengthened with Seated Wrist Curls.

Obvious bodyweight-powered exercises are dips for the chest muscles; fingerboard pull-ups (use the fingertips so that the whole finger is strengthened, but cosset your tendons with at least two days' rest between sessions, to get the synovial fluids circulating round the joints again) and press-ups. These are cheaper to do at home than in a gym, and can also be weighted with a sack of climbing gear.

Off-season training should concentrate on building strength; on-season training will help maintain it. Clearly, this chapter of the book isn't intended as a stand-in for a proper training programme. (My own off-season programme is given briefly on p. 152 – but don't use it as a basis to start from!) Your local gym or sports centre will design and supervize a programme of resistance training if you describe your needs.

They can also advise about food, as important for successful training as the work itself. Eat to reduce body-fat, which is useless to climbers. But beware. Climbers are by nature obsessive, and will sign up at the drop of a hat for a really exciting new behaviour pattern. There are several cases of climbers who – attempting to improve power-weight ratio by working on both sides of the equation at once – have induced anorexia nervosa (compulsive starving) in themselves. Avoid this kind of thing if you can. Anorexia is hard to cure; and malnutrition can lead to a severe drop in performance. A climbing diet should include 70% complex carbohydrate, 15% protein and 15% fats.

Training will tire you out. The correct response to this is to go to sleep at night, not party until dawn, especially if you intend climbing the next day. Insufficient rest leads to injury and reduced training-effect. On the crag, tiredness destroys agility, sense of balance and confidence.

Flexibility
While there are some basic skeletal brakes on movement, or we'd all flop about like puppets, the major

Kicking high: an exercise for flexibility.

Dancing promotes the suppleness and flexibility needed for climbing, and can be an ideal warming up exercise.

limitations on flexibility are soft-tissue limitations. Ligaments, which hold the joints together, tendons, which attach muscle to bone, and the muscles themselves, will only allow you so much movement. Other limits to flexibility are age – though this shows up mainly in people who have never tried to keep themselves mobile or flexible in the first place – look at the way an ageing dancer or Alexander Technique trainer moves, – and sex, women being more supple than men. (It's not clear whether this is a biological or a cultural condition. It seems likely though that while we are encouraging girls to move 'gracefully', we teach boys a type of movement which shortens the muscles and sets strength and explosive power above suppleness.)

Soft tissue can be stretched. Training for flexibility means increasing the length of the connective tissue while encouraging muscle tissue to relax. 'Ballistic' stretching, which involves pushing the muscle suddenly past its comfortable range of movement, leads to stiffness and injury, and is the main reason that generations trained on 'physical jerks' were neither very flexible nor very interested in sport as adults. 'Static' or 'passive' stretching in which the joints are brought gradually towards their movement-limits, is much safer and more efficient. Move to the point where some slight discomfort is felt, but never strain. Hold the position for ten to thirty seconds. Gentle stretching like

this can be done at home, as part of a warm-up, or after climbing when it will reduce next-day stiffness. Stretch at least three times a week; daily is best.

Some climbers work well on their nerves: they like to be sharp and psyched-up before a hard route. To others, this condition is exhausting, and a danger. Stretching has the valuable side-effect of reducing psychological as well as physical tightness, promoting a more relaxed approach – another gain in the area of 'head' skills. Don't develop flexibility without working on strength too: over-mobile joints need stronger muscles to hold the working parts in proper alignment to one another.

to stand upright and walk. A movement at first under complete conscious control becomes by practice progressively more automatic. But work on agility and coordination will cross over, and some climbers now play basketball to develop these skills. Team games are a rather bigger break with tradition than pre-placed bolt protection.

The Great Western Bouldering Competition.

Hands-off resting on a gritstone wall.

Balance, Co-ordination, Agility

As we've said, women have a lower centre of gravity than men: but this does not automatically bestow a better 'sense of balance'. Sense of balance is a feedback loop between the 'spirit levels' of the inner ear and the central nervous system. It is best trained by performing acts of balance. In Yosemite, US climbers set up a length of slack chain between two trees and walk along it like circus performers. You might do some balance-beam exercises. But otherwise, the best training for balance climbing is balance climbing, on boulders.

Agility is the control of the moving centre of gravity. Like co-ordination and sense of balance, it is a fuzzy concept, a complex function of the sensory motor system which can be trained only by repetition of specific movements – 'wiring' – the way a child learns

BOULDERING

Introduction

The Victorians did it. Nail scratches are the mute evidence. They did it at Laddow Rocks and Castlenaze in the Peak District, at Almscliffe in Yorkshire, at Wasdale Head and in Ogwen. The Edwardians did it, inside and outside public houses, in gym shoes. There was a guide to the Helyg Boulder before Menlove Edwards did it there. There are pictures of O. G. Jones and the Abrahams brothers doing it on a barn. It was done upside down and by women, *en masse* and as a solitary practice, and there are pictures of that too. Stanley Jeffcoat did it in bare feet on routes now graded VS. Bouldering can never really be separated from the early history of climbing.

Bouldering is a social event. You associate it with evening sunshine after work, and groups of people looking up at the rock. They are giving advice, having a crack, waiting for their turn. From the start bouldering

was a livelier, a gamier and more competitive way of doing the sport, and by the Brown era it had become one among several carefully-disguised forms of training. Problem areas like *Joe's Slab* on Froggatt were developed as outdoor gymnasia. Later, the PA – designed for boulders – took Fontainebleau all over Britain, where it assumed forms and faces grimmer than its origins on the ladylike sandstone of the Weald – abandoned quarries in Yorkshire and Lancashire where the scenery is less sacred than the move. Into this genetic mix were stirred rumours of the American boulders, especially John Gill, already legendary for his dedication, boredom with climbs, his one-finger pull-ups. Modern bouldering awaited only chalk to be born.

'Mountains,' Andy Woodward claimed in 1974, 'are only training for boulders.'

Originally designed as a teaching aid, with enormous holds and belay platforms, indoor climbing walls weren't much good for anything else until Don Robinson began to build them with inset natural stone. The Leeds University wall was probably the most crucial of these. It encouraged all-year-round bouldering in warm dry conditions, and immediately fostered a generation of technically-oriented climbers like Al Manson and John Syrett, who had hardly ever seen a crag but were able to *begin* on *Wall of Horrors*, Almscliffe. Their attitude to technique is the direct ancestor of the ultra-modern hard route.

Though indoor walls are now central to the climbing as well as the training experience, they have drawbacks which boulders do not. They cost money to use, they become very crowded in the evenings. Heavy traffic has polished them like glass. They are often hedged about with rules and their use circumscribed by sports centre management, which doesn't recognize a 'minority' sport without a distinct rule-based hierarchy. (The Sobell Wall in Islington, North London, suffers most of these problems and in addition is placed in a corridor along which toddlers are allowed to wander every afternoon.) Erosion is another problem, and some walls now have loose and broken holds.

A scrubbing brush and water will get caked chalk out of the pores of the stones. Wire brushes will roughen it up. But the only remedy for real polish is stone-cleaning fluid. Ask your sports centre management to invest in some and paint it on. Any builders' wholesaler will stock it. It's corrosive in use but quite harmless afterwards. A proper cleaning policy will then *keep* the stone free of polish.

Nat Allen and Joe Brown bouldering at Cromford Black Rocks.

Joe Brown at Bamford.

Bouldering the bottom of *Mint 400*, Froggatt.

So High, Joshua Tree: the most perfect boulder in the world.

Competitive bouldering

In the winter of 1984 I went through California on the way back from Japan. They were holding the Great Western Bouldering Competition at Mount Rubidoux, Joshua Tree. Rubidoux is a hill stuck up on a vast plain from which all you can see is the smog of Los Angeles. On the day there was a battery-powered computer set up in the car park. You turned up and paid a dollar, for which you got a map of the area marked with 200 problems graded from 1 to 20, and a score card with eleven slots.

Every boulder was surrounded with a crowd of competitors, spectators and TV cameramen. Somewhere in the middle of this melee stood a judge with a stopwatch, overseeing perhaps a dozen problems! The stopwatch started: you had three minutes: if you were still on the ground at the end of it, no score.

I'd had such an epic trying to find somewhere to sleep the night before, I wasn't sure where I was. I sat around knackered for about three hours after I got my entry form and score card, drinking coffee and chatting to people. It got to dinnertime and I hadn't even started. I decided to run between the problems. All the hot-shots were there. 'Show us your card. What have you done? Not *that*?' I managed a couple of 17s and decided to carry on. You could afford to try and fail on something really hard because your lowest score was scrubbed: but two zeroes and you were finished. I attracted one by trying a 20 (they turned out to be impossible) but I could hear people saying, 'Ron's doing really well. He's

Wild overhang moves on the boulders at Almscliffe.

in with a chance.' Then a couple of the big favourites collected a second zero each and gave up. It was getting late, and I needed one more problem . . .

What I found was a slab which seemed to be popular with the locals. It looked about V Diff, until you tried to do it. The rock was like glass: no friction at all. Even Firé rubber needed dabbing with alcohol or acetone or something, to make it stick, but I didn't find that out till later. All I knew was that my time was running out, and I'd been sandbagged. The judge's boyfriend had just done it and she was grinning at me and counting down – 'Two minutes fifteen, two minutes thirty, two . . .' I tried everything, but I'd blown it. The Germans and Japanese who had been following me around cheering had gone quiet, the locals were laughing, I had about two seconds left. In the end I just took a run at it, jumped off a little rock in front, hit the slab about halfway up and started to swim . . .

Not much technique there, admittedly, but I got to the top.

Training

That was a really good day out. Everyone enjoyed themselves. The youngest competitor was seven years old, the oldest a woman of 63. I didn't even know I'd won until they called my name out.

What is a boulder problem? Classically, it's a difficult move or series of moves done low enough down not to injure yourself if you fall off it. Like every other distinction in modern climbing, this is now breaking up, and new definitions are emerging. There are problems so awkward that you are going to fall off sideways or upside down, which is dangerous even at moderate heights; or with such bad landings that damage is hard to avoid: while 'high' bouldering means you can find yourself doing hair-raising stuff ten or fifteen metres up – on an outcrop, many problems of this sort would be fully-fledged routes.

It's easier to say where (good bouldering patches must be easily accessible for an evening visit, or a couple of hours when an otherwise wet weekend dries up), how (without ropes or equipment, because the absolute essence of bouldering is freedom of movement) and above all *why* you do it. Bouldering improves your strength and stamina, your technique, your judgement, and your courage. It stresses the parts that other forms of training cannot reach. Using a miniature local venue you can model many of the demands made on the climber by a full-size crag or a full-size panic.

Choose your landing.

Spotting for *Wall of Horrors,* Almscliffe (right).

Endurance and training

The commonest method of endurance training is to traverse to exhaustion at low-level then rest and traverse again. Since it mimics the 'real' situation of the climber, it comes under the rubric 'Climbing is the best training for climbing.'

There are some points to watch. The use of very small holds on steep rock – or of the brick edges of an indoor climbing wall – will make for stronger fingers. But if you want to pump the rest of your muscles you will have to find some other way of doing it. Secondly, there are other ways of using your muscles than simple reach-and-pull; low level traversing should test these too – otherwise it becomes boring as well as of limited use. Thirdly some of the effect will be undercut by the very fact that you are traversing. You tend, especially once you've learned a traverse, to fall or swing sideways. This is good for flexibility and reach, but it doesn't stress your muscles in the way they are stresses by climbing up and down, against gravity rather than utilizing it.

You can alleviate all these problems, especially boredom, by devising circuits which make use of features such as overhangs, roofs and so on. Most good walls already have established circuits – a good example is the 'underpass' at the Richard Dunn centre in Bradford – but if the wall you use is short of features you still don't have to be tied to traversing: go in loops and zigzags, a few moves up, a few moves back, a few moves down again. Variety is the key. Don't limit yourself to finger holds either – palming a very steep hold will pump the bigger muscles.

Eventually you will have a circuit so wired that it ceases to stress you. At this point a weight belt comes in useful. Start with three or four kilos. Take care not to do explosive moves with a weight belt, or moves which are new to you and might cause you to lurch or slip: it will wreck your tendons. There is some evidence that while weighted traversing increases strength it doesn't actually increase stamina. Some people like to wear their oldest, most knackered pair of boots to traverse in – this improves your footwork (if only by contrast when you get a decent pair on!) and puts more weight on your arms; or they wear trainers. Many climbing walls are so polished this is unnecessary.

Isometric strength and endurance can be useful for placing or removing protection, or in any situation where you have to stop and take stock: so if you rest during a training traverse, rest on the wall itself – using a bridge, holding yourself in with one arm while shaking out the other, or whatever.

Syrett's Overhang, Almscliffe, a power problem.

Traverse right from here for as long as you can!

Here the foot has to go on to the same hold as the fingers . . .

A long reach.

Radical technical moves on *Opus*, Almscliffe.

Bouldering for technique

Historically, bouldering is concerned with technique. Kept as fit as butchers' dogs by the weight of their ironmongery, big boots and ex-WD camping equipment, by long walk-ins and day-jobs as plumbers' mates, the Rock & Ice Club used the boulders to extend their technical vocabulary. Over in the US, John Gill was interested only in the move – he trained for the boulders, not on them. The US system of boulder grading is essentially technical. B1 begins where the hardest climbs leave off. A B3 is a problem which has had only one ascent. The moment anyone – even its originator – repeats it, it is downgraded to B2. Over here we grade problems in numerical grade only, as a signal that their technical difficulty is what counts.

Bouldering enables you to attack, defeat and then wire moves that were originally too hard for you. At a popular venue, the groups standing in front of the heavily chalked holds will show you where the hard problems are; the friendly competition will spur you on. Start out at your own level of skill, at around the grades you would expect to be able to top-rope. (Top roping is no substitute for bouldering, although it can be useful for endurance training.)

Squeak your boots. If the ground is wet or muddy, use a towel to step off: no one will thank you for muddying the footholds. The boulders are Chalk City, but be sensible. Chalk doesn't improve the performance of butyl rubber – quite the reverse. At weekends in the Peak I see holds chalked a few centimetres off the ground. More dwarfs must be climbing than I thought. Chalking a wet hold to dry it will leave you with a sticky paste useful for curing stomach upsets. I use a toothbrush to scour this mess off. Ask someone to watch your back, especially on overhangs; two spotters might be necessary for an awkward fall. Check your landing, and if it's uneven do some landscape gardening.

There are two ways of solving a boulder problem. You can learn the moves from someone else then practice them until you can do them all; or you can work on the problem in isolation, trying out methods of your own until you hit one that works. You'll learn faster by mixing these two methods. The Numbers can be used to build a basic repertoire, but personal solutions encourage inventiveness. You won't know the Numbers of every route you encounter. Who, anyway, climbs just to repeat other people's moves?

Psycho, Caley Crag: 6b moves on a big boulder.

A VS problem at Caley Crag – *Hanging Groove.*

Psychological aspects

Determination, mental and emotional stamina, courage and the ability to make decisions under stress, are central requirements for the climber. Boldness must be tempered by careful assessment, over-caution side-stepped by nerve. Adrenalin by-products give you a buzz, but they have to be controlled. There are two ways of shaking yourself off a small hold – out of fear, and out of sheer excitement. Neither is productive. Climbing is a kind of mental judo you do to yourself, to keep the body operating like a machine while confusion reigns elsewhere.

Bouldering – especially high bouldering on outcrops, which in its more radical forms is barely distinguishable from soloing – is the ideal way to assess, develop and train your psychological and motivational skills. Work up to it carefully, starting low and balancing increased height against technical difficulty and strenuosness. Other than climbing, this is the most dangerous thing you will take on: never rush yourself, or start out tired. Warm up on easy solos, to 'get your head in'. Approach the crucial moves of a problem by increments, checking out the escape routes, reversing off. You are learning to recognize your own limits – This is too high . . . This is too exposed . . . This is too hard without protection –

and then very slowly and carefully extend them, just like a stretching exercise.

You are aiming at calm familiarity with the rock, and with yourself. Considerable confidence is necessary to begin this process, and I wouldn't recommend it to every climber. It will help to start in company, especially with someone perhaps a bit more experienced and skilful. But the payback from this kind of training increases the more you climb on your own, even on low-level traverses. Being wholly responsible for yourself encourages a realistic assessment of what you can and can't do: and the very realization that no one will be there to help you if you fall can bring about a considerable strengthening of your will.

Physical training for climbing is still in its infancy, though climbers have been tackling rocks for over a hundred years: psychological training is an even newer idea. Climbers have traditionally used methods like these to back up their technique and fitness, though soloing and solitary climbing have also been periodically dismissed as 'unjustifiable'. As yet there seems no way in which they could be codified into a supplementary programme – there's no equivalent of weight-training for the mind!

A seven metre fall onto your back if you fall here. . .

Strenuous work on limestone pockets.

Fun

Bouldering was developed at Fontainebleau, just outside Paris, at the turn of the century. The boulders are very hard sandstone in a beautiful wooded environment – good friction, sandy landings. It's so accessible that the Parisians go bouldering the same way they play tennis. They don't even consider themselves climbers: this is a sport in itself. At weekends chic Parisian Ferraris roll up, out get chic Parisian couples who strip off, don shorts and follow the same colour-coded circuits from boulder to boulder. It's very French, formal and light at the same time, elegant, subtle and fashion-co-ordinated.

This is a far cry from Sunday afternoon at Greetland Quarry in Halifax, known to the locals as the 'pigshit quarry' because of the drainage from the farm above. Favoured clothing there in the nippier weather is likely to be a quilted car-coat and a pair of trousers given you by John Hart's father. But the message is the same. Bouldering is fun. You aren't tied up in a lot of ropes. You can boulder out of a car-park; or throw your boots in a bag and run ten km to some sunny outcrop and see no-one all afternoon. The best boulders have distinct lines of their own, like micro-crags (eliminating holds to make a problem might be good discipline, but it's not somehow in the spirit of the thing) and they are situated somewhere like the Bridestones near Hebden Bridge, where you can sit down when you're tired and stare out across all the moorland in the world.

BUILDERING

In sharp contrast again is the urban sport of buildering. This has hallowed roots in cat-burglary and the undergraduate climbing of university buildings. All things decline though, and from a gesture of bravado, buildering – in Britain anyway – has modified itself into a convenient form of training for those trapped far from crags.

It can be done on any kind of structure, although banks, government buildings and bonded warehouses are not recommended. Brick and stone walls provide excellent finger training. Concrete expansion slots can be jammed. Bridges and the high walls of canals and motorways are favoured spots – don't take more than a step backwards at the bottom of the latter. Be wary of old, rotten brickwork, and have a story ready for the police. At the end of the day's buildering you are more likely to watch the sun go down over Euston than Wharfedale, but at least you can go and have a Macdonalds.

In America, a much glossier form of buildering has developed, in which, using carefully designed equipment to make use of window-cleaning flanges and other structural features, very tall buildings can be climbed. Though glamorous, and often seen on TV news, this is definitely aid-climbing.

Deceptive overhanging rock at Caley, Yorkshire.

Conclusion

Nothing gives you confidence like technique. But to do what?

The original, Victorian values of rock climbing were second hand. They leaked in from a different activity – mountaineering – and put a high premium on wilderness travel, isolation from the social world, hardship, and objective risk (we've seen how the last-named was preserved and increased by the equipment of the day, the limitations of which themselves became a value enshrined as 'the leader never falls'). They were, in short, exploratory. It's in order even now to describe your Himalayan holiday as an 'expedition' – especially to your sponsors, if you can find any Chris Bonington hasn't used up – as if something unknown, and of unknown significance, remains to be ear-holed out of the world above seven thousand metres, some final morsel of geographical knowledge prised out of the glaciers or extracted from the weather patterns.

Go where no one has even been before. Find out what it's like to be there. Send back reports – 'Magnetic anomalies affected our compass . . . at sunset, behind the Col Mirador.' 'Reaching for objects I sometimes found my hands grasping nothing.'

This became, by definition, decreasingly possible. Geography is a non-renewable resource. Returns diminished as the great ranges, the great adventures, were worked out. The moment you repeat someone else's great adventure you have introduced an element of the artificial: you have invented a sport. What was a discovery in an absolute sense – the North Pole, the South Pole, the summit of Everest – becomes only a personal investigation. Hermann Buhl finds his Annapurna sanctuary only the once. After that his drama of self-expression is quickly codified, becomes a game (if a dangerous one), and we have something closer to the Wandervogel adventures of Gwen Moffat in Wales after the Second World War, beautifully preserved, beautifully honest, but nonetheless bijou:

> After the climb we were delightfully tired. Already that day we had done several routes, and when we reached the top of Glyder Fach, where the big flat boulders were hot under the afternoon sun, we stretched out like animals and went to sleep. After a while we awoke and felt hungry, and we came down Bristly Ridge with our last spurt of energy. By the time we reached the tents we were staggering, and we sank on the grass and slept again – until midnight, when we cooked a meal by the light of our torches, while owls called and stars glittered above the larch wood.
>
> (*Space Below My Feet*, 1961)

So it goes. There's nothing wrong with it. The ancestral line remains, linking public and private voyages of experience, great myths and small ones, secret gardens and municipal parks. But you would be hard put to experience Bristly Ridge that way nowadays, and at Stanage Edge on a Saturday afternoon you can no longer convince yourself by any means that the sanctuary is your own. 'Turn that bloody radio off, Derek!' the teachers call to their school parties: 'You're supposed to be out for a day in the country!' You are climbing with – and sometimes on – a thousand other people. Even on a weekday, two minutes after you have arrived in the middle of a completely empty crag, someone from Birmingham comes and sits at the bottom of your route and asks you if you're going to be finished soon. At this point every climb becomes an eliminate, you are having to pretend so many things aren't there.

By the old values, you are allowed one last valid form of 'exploration': the new route. In Britain, this is a miniaturization of Buhl's frisson, it's true – but in a way the small scale and ephemerality of the experience makes it more not less intense. Whatever else, anyway, at least nobody has been *here* before you.

Only yourself.

BETWEEN THE DESIRED AND THE POSSIBLE

Unclimbed rock being a dwindling commodity, any new route is likely to be so strenuous, so technically demanding, so inaccessible to traditional methods of climbing, that before you can lead it you must already be on familiar terms with it. You notice a possible line: you inspect it by abseil, it looks as if it will go: cleaning it, you abseil down it again repeatedly. You place a bolt, practise a move or two. It's a long, intimate foreplay between the two of you. By the time you consummate, by the time you red-point, you might have been down the line forty times. You've been falling off parts of it for a month. You might even have practised it, move by move, from the top downwards. Without this intimacy you are simply not going to get up it.

Modern lines are invented. We ran out of the more obvious features to follow long ago – the slab blurs into the wall, the wall impends – and a 'line of weakness' now is only a stitching-together of technical possibilities made possible by the imagination and commitment of the first-ascentionist. Its risk factor is equally a value judgement – when we talk about a 'sporting' bolt placement, we are admitting that someone has *chosen* what was once left up to nature. We make our own lines now. I see no loss in this. It was a process that began when the first sport-climber tied on to a rope. Ideally, we would flash all lines on sight. But we aren't 'naked

Everything is up for grabs.

before the crag', and we never were. That's a lie we tell to pretend that climbing is somehow both meaningful and 'natural', when actually – like a crossword puzzle – it's a game we've made up, the rules of which we could change whenever we wanted to.

What messages can we send back from today's explorations, then? 'Base camp is a bus stop outside Sheffield'? 'Whenever we tire we are playing the Big Audio Dynamite tape. It seems to help'? 'I did the crux of *Ulysses or Bust* four times, and I really like it'?

To be honest, I don't see why not.

We can retain the exploratory value of rock climbing – this sense of it being a 'real' encounter with a natural world – only so long as we understand that our adventures are purely personal; that they are cameos, re-enactments of more powerful myths. But if – as we look round at the old bedsteads and burned-out cars dumped at the bottom of Millstone Edge (or even think about what the description 'Millstone' implies) – this value has begun to seem rickety and absurd to us, then we shall need something to replace it with.

One alternative I've already suggested is the sheer pleasure of movement. Climbers climb to climb, not to get to the top. Fun like this is an infinitely renewable resource, unaffected by crowds, or even venues. A move is nicer in weather that cracks the flags on some lonely crag overlooking the sea; but it's just as pleasing *as a move* if you do it on an indoor wall in Bradford with the rain pissing down on the dual carriageway outside. We should learn, perhaps, to experience kinaesthetic-ally, as well as emotionally. It's a dance, a kind of pleasure that can be got at any grade in any circum-stances, the reason we all begin climbing. And if we brought it centre-stage, we would be putting a pre-mium on one of the absolute physical foundations of the sport. If I don't climb I get physical withdrawal symp-toms; I shake with muscle spasms; I need to *move*.

Equally, I feel much more mentally alive on a crag. It's my environment. My senses work overtime, fuelled by adrenalin. I'm out on the line between recklessness and control, and it's like a psychological addiction to go with the physical one. (Sometimes being so addicted frightens me. If I had a bad accident I could conceivably come to terms with the physical limitations – but what would I find to do half so exciting as climbing?) Here's another value we might bring to the centre of the sport, a shift from the exploration of physical geography to the exploration of the internal geography of the climber. Climbing would be a machine for self-investigation, for determining one's own limits under stress. Soloing and high-bouldering climbers would live in the gap between the desired and the possible, a zone personally determined, constantly stretched and reshaped.

THE BLACK SHEEP OF THE FAMILY

A third possibility is the competitive ethic. The Great Western Bouldering Championship mimicked in an organized way that sense of friendly competition you always feel on the boulders. In Italy I entered another kind of contest altogether.

This was strange, stressful, deeply professional stuff, a long way removed from 'real' climbing. (Of course it's actually no more or less real in its own way than any of the games climbers play. If its goals and values are different from those of – say – pure Alpine climbing, so are the rules and rewards of climbing in Flying Shed Quarry in Lancashire on a Monday evening after work!)

Contests of this sort take place in an arena, with big audiences, sponsorship, and television coverage from six different countries. You can feel the tension the moment you start to lead the first, easy, route, at around English 6a: you're in a space wholly unfamiliar

A debilitating technicality. *Oedipus Ring Your Mother*, E4 6a, Froggatt Edge.

Base Camp is a bus stop outside Sheffield, for *Paxo*, E6 6b, Raven Tor.

to British climbers, competition space, like a new kind of exposure yawning away at the back of your neck. The organizers pick a new crag each time – imagine having that much unclimbed rock! – then clean and bolt it and leave it to the contestants. You're timed and given points for style. Two hundred climbers start out: in forty eight hours a hundred and ninety of them are eliminated. Every time you look up someone is wrong-footing himself and getting slaughtered.

The final route comes in at E6 6b, an on-sight lead manufactured especially for the occasion. A tie will be decided on time and style. The judges are all French, which skews the definition of style – this will be cured by having international juries. I'd imagined it would be boring to watch, but the tension is incredible, it has all the hallmarks of watching someone else's gripper, a real spectator sport. On the last day the remaining competitors aren't allowed to see the two routes they're going to climb. There's a walkway taped off through the spectators to a belay area at the bottom of the crag. Over the megaphone you hear, 'Now we have Ron Fawcett, Contestant 123,' followed by a sort of career-precis, and you have to come down the walkway with the audience staring at you and tie on. It's terrifying. All the cameras are firing off. Three thousand people are watching you live, God knows how many on TV, and they count you down, '5, 4, 3, 2, 1, CLIMB!' and you fall off on the first move and that's that.

This sort of climbing is going to breed some very special skills. A couple of the French, good climbers but not massively good, always do well at competitions because having an audience brings out the best in them. Other, really excellent, climbers do less well because they're overawed and psyched-out by the circumstances. It's not so different, when you come to think of it, from some of the more traditional pressures of climbing. There's always some poor devil called Steve having an epic on a VS in Yarncliffe Quarry on a Sunday afternoon in front of fifty other climbers who've come down from Stanage to get out of the wind – lowering off his top runner, cracking up, failing to see huge ledges in front of his nose because everyone's looking at him and he knows they feel sorry for him and ashamed of him at the same time.

More serious is the kind of psyching-up you have to do for a hard new route. Like a boxer before a big fight, or a powerlifter in front of a big weight, you must achieve a balance between aggression and calm. Adrenalin and excitement will push you up the climb, but they will make it hard to think clearly; an absolute, steely determination will get you through an intimidating crux, but determination like that will tense your shoulders, tighten your muscles and reduce your flexibility; utter commitment is one thing, but that the

Americans call 'the inner game', that ability to call freely on your unconscious rather than conscious skills, is quite another. Over the years, individual climbers have developed various versions of Zen, or yoga, or mediation, to try and cope with this conflict. I often go for a short run, after I've psyched-up but before I start out on the route: this seems to relax me and enables me to direct the nervous energy I've generated.

Directing – or redirecting – nervous energy en route is another problem. Climbers often shake themselves off small holds out of sheer excitement. Here, the best plan is to try and climb quickly, keep moving, tap your reserves of deft, fluid movement. I sometimes hear my own voice murmuring, 'No pain no gain,' or 'Come on arms, do your stuff,' like a mantra, and I wonder if this is a way of steadying myself down. Psyching-down again after a successful climb is less of a difficulty. For hours afterwards you're lapped in adrenalin breakdown chemicals, high as a kite on achievement – pure luxury!

LOOKING PROFESSIONALISM IN THE FACE

Achievement is as much a value as a kick; and personal achievement as worthwhile a value as public achievement. It is maintained throughout the grades, from Diff to E8. We all like to surpass ourselves. For the committed rock climber, though, this means a desperate and often demoralizing struggle to buy time – time in which to train, to practise, to add to that vital technical vocabulary on rock worldwide. I realize that in the present state of opinion only the black sheep of the British family brings up the subject of competition climbing. But outside Britain, British climbers find themselves looking professionalism in the face. Good lads like Ben Moon and Martin Atkinson stare a bit sadly and enviously at their Continental peers. Anyone who wants to make a living out of what he does best – and in the process buy time to do it better, because who else will buy it for him? – is going to have to get out into that arena and compete.

Professional climbing in Britain is, apart from the odd exotic moment, an altogether dourer way of earning a living than dancing for it high up in front of an audience. It's a bread and butter job. I wanted to be a professional – in the sense that I wanted to climb to live so I could live to climb – from the first day I got off the ground, but sometimes, driving between small northern towns in the rain on my way to act as a sales-rep for my sponsor, I wonder why. The moors are always clagged in, the car parks are always full, and the Fiesta is always making a new noise when you change down into second. Climbing hard routes isn't in the job description. If you work for yourself you're at work twenty-four hours a day, seven days a week. When the telephone rings it might be an offer of a few days

The exploratory value: looking for it on Stanage Edge.

employment 'minding' a film cameraman on a mountain in Switzerland (I've ended up working the camera myself, because the cameraman had less of a head for heights than he claimed he had), or as an actor's stand-in for a programme about a dead climber. But it's more likely to be to finalize the details of an eight-day stint behind a counter at a trade show, with your muscles sagging and your brain turning to jelly as you stand there demonstrating boots.

'See? We've got a rounded toe on these, for better toe-tip edging.'

This hardly matters against the need to climb. In fact it doesn't matter at all. I pull out of the top of a new route at Gordale or Raven Tor with a shout of elation and release, all that work, all the falls I've ever taken, bones I've ever broken, red-pointed into one intense, fluid experience, knowing immediately I'm not going to be able to describe any of it, only repeat in a kind of mad rage what I already know, what I've known since I was fifteen –

'It's fantastic, it's fucking fantastic!'

Other times, climbing throws you into the heart of your own life, which is the only thing that ever matters. To know what this book has really been about – because technique, like professionalism, is only a means to an end – get up early on a Saturday morning at the beginning of May. Walk down the Manifold Valley to the bottom of Beeston Tor. A jackdaw circles out from the rock. On the steep, deteriorating terraces below, white thorn-blossom is massing on the bare black branches. Everything is coming out of the thermal lag of the winter. Stand there with the sunshine beginning to warm your back, listen for the noises of the valley as it wakes up – a woodpecker that sounds like a toy gun, a footstep in the dry river bed. Think of all the things you have had to do in the week so that you can be here now. Then slowly reach out and touch the rock with the flat of your hand. Let it lead your eye upwards. There. You're alive again.

Between the desired and the possible. The gap yawns at Rheinstor.

Ron soloing down *Rubberneck*, Five Clouds, The Roaches.

Favourite Climbs

Being an avid 'boulderer', some of my favourite areas fall into this category. Sadly, my adopted home of the Peak District has a distinct lack of good bouldering. To me, good bouldering has purity of line and independence, as epitomized by the magical Caley boulders or the mysteries of Earl Crag's West End or the Brownstones. Sadly, we have no Fontainebleau's or Joshua Trees hidden away behind some South Yorkshire heap, but we survive.

As for routes, my favourite rock is undoubtedly limestone: I love the complexity and variation coupled with the angle, which is usually 'steep'. Here in the UK our limestone is rather inferior to that of our European neighbours and hence a list of favourites should include the greats of Buoux and Verdon – but this would go on forever. What we do have in the UK, which is lacking somewhat in Europe, is history, character, and a wealth of great climbing – if only we had the weather!

LIST OF ROUTES
Sustained
The Prow, E6 6b 6b 6b, Raven Tor; Eye of the Tiger, E6 6b, Dovedale; Cave Route Lefthand E6 6c, Pierrepoint E7 6c 6b, Hangman E6 6b 6a, all at Gordale; Free and Easy E6 6c, Zoolook E7 6c, Raindogs E7 6b, all at Malham Cove; Hollywood Bowl, E6 6c, Giggleswick Scar; Guadeloupe, E5 6b, Loup Scar; Dominatrix, E6 6b, Kilnsey; Lord of the Flies, E6 6a, Dinas Cromlech; Manic Strain, E7 6b, Vivian Quarry; Strawberries, E6 6b, Tremadoc; Hell's Wall, E6 6c, Borrowdale; Cumbrian, E6 6b, Esk Buttress; White Heat, E6 6c, Pembroke.

Explosive Power
Revelations, E7 6c, Raven Tor; Kudos, E7 6c, Water Cum Jolly; Maximum, E6 6c, and New Dawn, E6 6c, Malham Cove.

Slabs
I have never been an avid slab climber, but every now and again I have to purge the system and go for it.

Slip and Slide, E6 6b, Crookrise; Shirleys Shining Temple, E4 6c, Stanage; Great Slab, E3 5b, and Hairless Heart, E5 5c, Froggatt Edge; Doris's Route, Difficult, Ilkley; Naked Before the Beast, E6 6b. Rainbow of Recalcitrance, E6 6b, Stiff Syd's Cap, E6 6b, all at Rainbow Slab; Flashdance/Belldance, E6 6b, Vivian Quarry.

Cracks
The granite of Yosemite has got to be one of the finest crack infested areas in the world. To pick out individual favourites is rather unfair on the rest, but I have to mention The Phoenix, 5.13; several pitches on Astroman, 5.11, Tales of Power, 5.12, Crimson Cringe, 5.11 – I could go on forever.

Here in the UK, my limited choice would be: London Wall, E5 6b, Millstone Edge; Wellington Crack, E5 6b, and Milky Way, E6 6b, Ilkley; Atomic Hot Rod, E6 6b, Dinas Cromlech; Requiem, E6 6b, Dunbarton Rock; Reticent Mass Murderer, E5 6b, Cratcliffe Tor.

Training Routine

(Dependent on work commitment.)

WINTER

10.00 – 11.30	Workout in gym. Weight machines – bench presses, lat. machines Pull-downs, pulley-rowing Stretching – leg work Inclined sit-ups Pull-ups – 10 sets of 20
Dependent on weather	Bouldering – e.g. Froggatt for 2 hours
or, if bad weather	Run on fells, up to 8 or 9 miles.
Evenings	Pull-ups at home, stretching, or a short, hard run.

SUMMER

Climbing or bouldering	Until I'm tired or my fingers are worn out Stretching Pull-ups – 10 sets of 20.

Acknowledgements

Thanks – from Ron

Early days with Paul Trower, Mick Hillas and Phil Webb – epics hitching, dossing in barns and then branching out. Geoff Birtles and Al Evans in Derbyshire. Pete Livesey, the competitor with joint sorties to Europe and the United States.

The 'SADCOCS' – Skipton and district climbing or caving society, especially Chris Gibb, the best climbing partner one could ever ask for. Brian Swales, Ian Dobson, Terry Birks – a great 'fun' team. Also, Paul Williams down in Wales. When travelling, meeting John Long in the States, Andreas Kubin, Wolfgang Gulich and Kurt Albert in Germany, Tatsuno and Kudon in Japan.

Thanks to Gill for the support, also to John for making this project possible, and to Mike for doing the 'words'. Finally, thanks Mum for putting up with me for all these years.

Mike Harrison's thanks go to Jane Johnson, who transcribed the tapes, and to Dennis and Lorna Mason at the Rose and Crown, Eyam, for their hospitality.

Unwin Hyman would like to thank Ron, John and Mike for all their work and enthusiasm in putting the book together; Jim Perrin for his introduction; Julian Holland, the book designer; Mr. Lawford of the Alpine Club Library for allowing us to use the picture on p. 106, left; and Nat Allen for permission to use the two photographs on page 130.

Index

(Numbers in italics refer to pictures or captions.
Names in italics refer to routes)